LIBEL AND THE MEDIA
The Chilling Effect

D0774485

WITHDRAWN

Libel and
the Media
The Chilling Effect

ERIC BARENDT, LAURENCE LUSTGARTEN,
KENNETH NORRIE and HUGH STEPHENSON

CLARENDON PRESS · OXFORD
1997

Oxford University Press, Great Clarendon Street, Oxford OX2 6DP

Oxford New York
Athens Auckland Bangkok Bogota Bombay
Buenos Aires Calcutta Cape Town Dar es Salaam
Delhi Florence Hong Kong Istanbul Karachi
Kuala Lumpur Madras Madrid Melbourne
Mexico City Nairobi Paris Singapore
Taipei Tokyo Toronto
and associated companies in
Berlin Ibadan

Oxford is a trade mark of Oxford University Press

Published in the United States
by Oxford University Press Inc., New York

© *E.M. Barendt, L. Lustgarten, K. Norrie and H. Stephenson 1997*

All rights reserved. No part of this publication may be reproduced,
stored in a retrieval system, or transmitted, in any form or by any means,
without the prior permission in writing of Oxford University Press.
Within the UK, exceptions are allowed in respect of any fair dealing for the
purpose of research or private study, or criticism or review, as permitted
under the Copyright, Designs and Patents Act, 1988, or in the case of
reprographic reproduction in accordance with the terms of the licences
issued by the Copyright Licensing Agency. Enquiries concerning
reproduction outside these terms and in other countries should be
sent to the Rights Department, Oxford University Press,
at the address above

This book is sold subject to the condition that it shall not, by way
of trade or otherwise, be lent, re-sold, hired out or otherwise circulated
without the publisher's prior consent in any form of binding or cover
other than that in which it is published and without a similar condition
including this condition being imposed on the subsequent purchaser

British Library Cataloguing in Publication Data
Data available

Library of Congress Cataloging in Publication Data
Data available
ISBN 0–19–826227–2
ISBN 0–19–826234–5 (pbk)

Typeset by Cambrian Typesetters Frimley, Surrey
Printed in Great Britain
on acid-free paper by
Biddles Ltd., Guildford and King's Lynn

KN
38
.21
L53

Preface

This book is a study of the impact of defamation law on various branches of the mass media in Great Britain. The media, particularly national newspapers, have long complained about the deleterious repercussions of this area of law for their work, arguing that frequently they are deterred through fear of libel proceedings from publishing material which should see the light of day. Our initial objective was to examine this claim, and to see whether the deterrent or 'chilling' effect of libel law applied equally to all branches of the media. However, the study is concerned to explore a wide range of other issues: what, for example, are the arrangements made by the media to handle libel risks, to what extent do they rely on outside legal advice, and how far do they seek insurance cover? Further, we wanted to find out whether defamation law is more or less significant to the media in Scotland compared with those south of the Border.

This is a study of an area of law which hitherto has been strangely neglected by both academic lawyers and by socio-legal scholars. As a consequence the agenda for law reform seems to have been drawn up almost exclusively by libel law practitioners and by the Lord Chancellor's Department. We hope that the results of our research will lead to wider and better informed discussion of the relationship between libel law and freedom of the media. We should however emphasize that further research is necessary, in particular into the costs of libel proceedings. In this context it is only right to add that none of us is an expert in socio-legal work, and we are conscious that other studies could add much to our account.

We are grateful to a number of institutions and individuals who made this research possible. In the first place, we are pleased to acknowledge the receipt of a grant from the Economic and Social

Research Council, which was of considerable assistance in meeting secretarial and other costs. In particular, it enabled us to employ a Research Assistant, Sheila Fahy, who conducted some of the interviews and who also spent many hours in the Royal Courts of Justice collecting statistics about the libel actions set down for trial in London. Her enthusiasm and support were always invigorating, and without her help we would have found it impossible to complete this research.

The Guild of Editors, Publishers Association, and Periodical Publishers Association were of great assistance in sending out questionnaires on our behalf, organizing meetings, or giving us access to their own surveys. We would like to thank by name Christopher Jones OBE (Chief Clerk, Central Office of the Royal Courts of Justice); David Newell, Santha Rasaiah, and Mary Russell of the Newspaper Society; Charles Clark and colleagues at the Publishers Association; and Peter Mason of the Periodical Publishers Association. More generally, we are grateful to the large number of newspaper, broadcasting, and other lawyers, journalists, editors, publishers, and others who assisted us by returning questionnaires and by sparing the time for interview. Finally, we would like to thank Sylvia Lough for the transcription of countless taped interviews and for invaluable administrative help.

The interviews for this study were for the most part conducted in 1994 and 1995. Our conclusions therefore cannot take full account of the impact of the changes to defamation law made by the Defamation Act 1996. Indeed, we finished the writing of this book in July 1996 as the Bill secured Royal Assent. Consequently, we have been able to mention some of its provisions in the first chapter of the book.

Eric Barendt prepared the drafts of Chapters 1 (with Kenneth Norrie), 2 (with Sheila Fahy), 4, 5, and 9 (with Laurence Lustgarten). Laurence Lustgarten and Hugh Stephenson wrote Chapter 3; in addition the former wrote Chapter 6, and the latter wrote Chapter 7. Kenneth Norrie wrote Chapter 8 on Scottish law. But we share responsibility for the final text and for any errors that may have been made in the presentation of our findings.

ERIC BARENDT
LAURENCE LUSTGARTEN
KENNETH NORRIE
HUGH STEPHENSON

July 1996
University College London

Contents

1

The Law of Defamation

Introduction

The law of defamation is notoriously complex. Although it is not easy to summarize its rules in a few pages, a short statement of English libel law is necessary in order to appreciate its impact on the various branches of the media which we describe in the following chapters. Exposition of these principles is particularly difficult at the time of writing (the summer of 1996), as some aspects of the law have recently been amended by the Defamation Act 1996. Some of the reforms contained in this measure are significant, particularly in the context of defamation procedure; they are referred to in this Chapter at the appropriate point. But they do not alter the main principles of the substantive law of libel. This Chapter also explains how the law and procedure in Scotland differ from those in England.

Obviously defamation law does not only affect newspapers, broadcasters, and publishers and the plaintiffs who sue them. Individuals, corporations, and partnerships may also be sued, if they publish a defamatory allegation (or in the case of a corporate defendant authorize its publication). This is illustrated by one of the most famous actions in the last decade, that brought by Lord Aldington against the author and distributor of a leaflet falsely accusing him of handing over prisoners of war to the Russians in the knowledge that this would lead to their death. This was in no sense a media case. But the vast majority of *causes célèbres* in defamation law do involve media defendants; plaintiffs naturally prefer to bring an action against them as well as, or instead of, an individual author, because the media are much more likely to be able to pay a significant award of damages. Further, they are the principal beneficiaries of the fair comment defence and the statutory qualified privilege for fair and accurate reports provided by the Defamation Act 1996, although in principle the former also covers private individuals (see pp. 10–15 below).

Two aspects of defamation law do not require any detailed treatment in the context of this book. As is well-known, English (though not Scots) law draws a distinction between libel and slander. The former may be defined as the publication of defamatory material in writing or in some other permanent form, while slander is its publication by oral means. The Defamation Act 1952, section 1 makes it plain that broadcast statements are to be treated as a publication in permanent form. So they must be regarded as potentially libellous. A defamation action in respect of publication by the media will therefore always be for libel rather than slander. The consequences of the difference between libel and slander will, therefore, not be explored in this book.[1] In fact, as there are relatively few actions for slander, the term 'libel' is often used when strictly the generic word 'defamation' would be more accurate; in this book the words are used interchangeably, although it should be remembered that outside the media context the difference between libel and slander may be important.

Secondly, the requirement in English law that the defamation be published will not be explored in detail. The victim of a defamatory allegation must show that it was published to a third party in order to succeed in a civil action for damages. (Such publication is not a necessary element of a criminal prosecution for libel, but we are not concerned with the crime in this study.) Obviously this gives rise to no difficulties in the case of newspapers, broadcasts, and other media publications. Consequently, there is little need here to discuss what constitutes

[1] The principal difference is that the law presumes that a libel damages the plaintiff, while the victim of slander, with some exceptions, has to prove that damage has occurred: see *Duncan & Neill on Defamation* (ed. by Sir Brian Neill and Richard Rampton, Butterworth, 2nd edn., London, 1983), ch. 3.

'publication', a matter which may be quite complex when the defendant is an individual.

What is Defamatory?

Libel law protects the right to reputation against defamatory allegations. But what exactly is *defamatory*? The courts have provided a number of definitions. At one time it was thought that a defamatory attack was one which held up the plaintiff to hatred, ridicule, or contempt. But that definition is now considered too narrow. A standard formulation is that of Lord Atkin in a House of Lords case in 1936. A defamatory publication is one which tends 'to lower the plaintiff in the estimation of right-thinking members of society generally'.[2] This definition makes it plain that the remarks must injure the individual's reputation in the eyes of reasonable members of the public, rather than a particular group. So it is almost certainly not defamatory to write of someone that he has reported criminals to the police, since that is regarded by most people as a praiseworthy thing to do.

In other respects, however, Lord Atkin's test is extremely vague. It is unclear, for example, whether it would be defamatory to say of someone that he or she is gay, has committed a very minor motoring offence, or is seriously ill with cancer. General abuse in a newspaper headline, or unfair treatment in an article or broadcast, does not usually amount to defamation, but there is always a risk that a specific unfavourable allegation will be regarded as defamatory. It is for the jury to decide the meaning of the words used in the article or broadcast and whether they are defamatory or not—though the judge may rule before the case comes to trial whether the words are capable of bearing a particular meaning alleged by one of the parties to the case.[3] The

---

[2] *Sim* v. *Stretch* [1936] 2 All ER 1237, 1240.

[3] Following recent changes to the Rules of Court governing High Court procedure in libel cases, either party has a right to apply to a judge for him to determine whether the words complained of are capable of bearing a particular meaning.

jury must decide what is the ordinary and natural meaning of the words, taking into account the context of the publication and any reasonable inferences which a normal reader, listener, or viewer would draw. Therefore, while it is uncertain whether it is libellous in the abstract to allege that someone is gay or bisexual, it may well be regarded as such in the particular context of the whole article or broadcast. Taken as a whole this claim might suggest that the person concerned, say, a popular entertainer, has misrepresented his sexuality and is therefore in this respect dishonest, or it might be regarded as libellous because it links his sexuality with his role in providing family entertainment.

The importance of considering an article or broadcast as a whole is illustrated by a recent decision of the House of Lords:[4]

The *News of the World* reported that a new computer game used the faces of well-known soap stars in conjunction with the bodies of porn actors. It published photos of the faces of two actors, who played characters in *Neighbours*, superimposed on the bodies of persons engaged in intercourse or sodomy. While the photos and the headline suggested the actors had posed for pornographic photos, the captions and full text made it plain that the actors' faces had been used without their consent.

The Lords affirmed the lower court decisions that the headline and photograph must be read together with the full article, and that, therefore, on these facts the plaintiff could not rely on the defamatory meaning which would be conveyed to those readers who only looked at the headline or the photograph. But that does not mean that a libellous headline or photograph will always be cured by the rest of an article; in some circumstances the ordinary reader may only take in the headlines, as, for example, when the bulk of the article is in small print or published on another page.

Occasionally an article or broadcast will appear totally harmless, but because of some special facts known to some readers or viewers will carry a defamatory meaning. A classic example of this would be a story associating someone with a particular property, known to a handful of people to be a brothel: that would be

---

[4] *Charleston and anor.* v. *News Group Newspapers Ltd.* [1995] 2 All ER 313.

defamatory because of what is known as an 'innuendo'. In these circumstances the plaintiff has to prove the special facts which make an otherwise innocent story defamatory. Since liability in defamation does not depend on proof of fault (see later, p. 6), the newspaper or broadcaster will not be able to argue that it was unaware of these special facts. Suppose, for instance, a news report or programme contained a shot of a public figure relaxing at a bar or hotel, and that the premises, unknown to the reporter and most people, were used for illegal gambling. The newspaper or broadcasting company might be liable for libel; it is quite immaterial that it did not know, and had no reason to know, the facts by virtue of which the report carried a libellous implication.

It is impossible to give precision to a concept as nebulous as 'the right to reputation'. What is defamatory must inevitably be defined in the circumstances of the particular case. Moreover, what will lower someone in the estimation of the public will vary from one generation to another. It is almost certainly no longer defamatory to suggest of someone that he or she has in the past had sexual liaisons before embarking on a current relationship—it may violate that person's privacy, but that as such is not actionable either in English or in Scots law. But the point is that one could not be sure there is no libel liability without knowing all the facts and the context in which the story is written. The vagueness of what constitutes a *defamatory* allegation is one reason why the media have to be on their guard.

Who Can and Does Sue for Libel?

Any living individual can, of course, sue for libel, whether the article or broadcast explicitly refers to him or not. The test is whether reasonable readers or viewers would believe that it refers to the plaintiff. Witnesses may be called to give evidence that they understood the allegations to concern him. In practice, in the absence of legal aid for libel actions, only the rich and those people who are supported by professional associations or other sponsors can afford to do so. It is common for professional bodies, such as the Police Federation, and to some extent trade unions, to provide financial backing for their members. Equally, corporations and other legal persons may sue, provided the defamation concerns their business; obviously a company cannot claim general damages for injury to its feelings. On the other hand, trade unions lack legal personality and so cannot sue. Recently, in *Derbyshire County Council v. Times Newspapers Ltd*[5] the House of Lords decided that a public authority cannot bring a libel action, because to allow it that capacity would inhibit freedom of political speech. The local authority's action in that case was, therefore, dismissed. It remains to be seen whether the principle established in the *Derbyshire* case will eventually be extended to public officials, so as to provide the media with some degree of immunity from libel suits (for further discussion of this point, see pp. 14–15 below).

In England the reputation of the dead cannot be protected by a civil action brought by a relative. Nor does an action for libel survive the death of either the plaintiff or, perhaps more anomalously, the defendant. Groups cannot protect their reputation. If a newspaper writes an article attacking financial greed at the Bar, no individual barrister could sue for libel. But the smaller the class and the more specific the allegation, the more likely it is that a jury could hold that it referred to the individual plaintiff.[6]

The Basis of Liability

The defendant may be liable for defamation, whether or not it was at fault. In other words, libel liability is strict. It is no defence to argue that the journalist (and editor) did not believe the article was defamatory and had no reason to believe it could be. Nor can the defendant argue that there was every reason to believe that the story was true and accurate in every detail. As we will see, it is for the defendant to prove the truth of the allegations to succeed in a

---

[5] [1993] AC 534.
[6] The leading case is *Knupffer* v. *London Express Newspaper Ltd* [1944] AC 116.

defence of justification, and if it is unable to do this it is just as liable as it would be if it had published the story maliciously.

There is even liability when a story is published which unintentionally refers to a person, even a person of whom the writer (and editor) has never heard. This rule was established in the famous case, *Hulton* v. *Jones*,[7] where the plaintiff, a barrister called Artemus Jones sued in respect of a sketch in a Sunday paper about a festival in Dieppe containing this sentence: 'There is Artemus Jones with a woman who is not his wife, who must be, you know,—the other thing!'. The newspaper's argument that it had concocted the name and knew nothing of the plaintiff was rejected by the House of Lords. It was perhaps a disingenuous argument since he had at one time worked for the newspaper, but the point of principle was established and has always been followed by the courts. The publisher takes the risk that the article (or film or broadcast) will be understood to refer to a particular person; she cannot argue that she did not intend to implicate the latter or did not know of his existence. This rule of libel law explains why newspapers always publish, when they can, the full names and addresses of parties to legal proceedings—to minimize the risk that a court report may be taken to refer to another person and so give rise to liability for 'unintentional defamation'. Broadcasters must be careful to avoid the use of film which, for example, depicts someone who is wholly uninvolved with the story.[8]

Who Can be Sued?

We have already pointed out that defamation liability is not confined to the media. Anyone who publishes a libellous allegation may be liable. Moreover, each person with responsibility for the publication is liable. This means that an action may be

---

[7] [1910] AC 20.

[8] In a well-known case Granada were required to pay £20,000 for an unintentional defamation when a *World in Action* investigation into police corruption inadvertently showed the plaintiff, an innocent but identifiable police officer, walking down the steps of a police station.

brought not only against the author of, say, a newspaper article, but also against the editor and proprietor of the paper, its printers and distributors, and the shop which sells it. (A reader who passes on a copy of the libellous article to a friend is also liable, though it is most improbable he would be sued, bearing in mind the range of media defendants to choose from.) Equally, every company involved in a broadcast may be liable—for example, an independent production company which makes the libellous programme, the broadcaster (say, the BBC or Channel 4) which incorporates the programme in its schedule, and, insofar as it is separate, the transmitting company. In practice, as will be explored in Chapter 5, the broadcaster assumes responsibility for ensuring the absence of defamatory allegations in a programme made by an independent producer and takes out insurance to cover the latter. Similar arrangements apply in book-publishing contracts. The publisher has the book checked for libel risks, and frequently insures the author for liability, though the contract often contains a rarely-enforced clause under which the author will indemnify the publisher for any libel damages and costs it occurs: see Chapter 6.

At common law a distributor of a book or newspaper enjoyed a special defence of 'innocent dissemination'.[9] A wholesaler, newsagent, bookseller, or library has not been liable, provided it did not know, and had no reason to believe, that the paper or book contained libellous matter. The Defamation Act 1996 extends this defence to everyone who does not have primary responsibility for a publication, that is those who are not authors, editors, and publishers. The protection now extends, for example, to broadcasters of live programmes with regard to statements over which they lack effective control, as well as, it seems, to internet service-providers.

However, the innocent dissemination defence, even after the new legislation, does not always exculpate distributors and booksellers. Once they have been put on notice by a potential plaintiff that the matter they are handling may contain defamatory

---

[9] The leading case is *Vizetelly* v. *Mudie's Select Library Ltd* [1900] 2 QB 170.

material, they can no longer claim that they are acting totally innocently. Moreover, in comparison with writers and editors, committed to the truth of their book or paper and freedom of expression, distributors are much less likely to attempt to defend libel actions for reasons of principle. Consequently, people contemplating the launch of libel proceedings against a newspaper, magazine, or book publisher may advise distributors to withdraw all copies of the 'offending' publication and take separate legal proceedings against them if they do not comply with this request. The late Robert Maxwell was particularly fond of this tactic. A distributors' settlement will not as a matter of law prejudice the rights of authors and publishers anxious to mount a defence of justification or fair comment (see later, pp. 10–12) but if widely reported may have an impact on public opinion and so encourage other parties to settle to the advantage of the plaintiff.

Defences

Naturally we are primarily concerned with the most important defences for media defendants. In general the same rules apply as to other defendants, though the press, magazines and broadcasting companies, and now book publishers, enjoy some special statutory defences under the Defamation Acts 1952–96. It is for the defendant to show on the balance of probabilities (the burden of proof in civil cases) that the defence is made out. For example, a newspaper or broadcaster must prove that the defamatory allegations are true or amount to fair comment or that they were made on a privileged occasion. That is because under the common law of libel defamatory allegations are presumed to be false and actionable. As we will see later (see p. 15), that is not always the case in other jurisdictions where the shape of libel law has recently been radically altered by constitutional restraints.

1. Justification

If the defendant proves that the defamatory allegations are true the action will fail. Justification, to use the legal term (*veritas in*

Scotland), is a complete defence in itself; the defendant does not have to show that it was in the public interest to publish the truth, as is the case with criminal libel and in some other jurisdictions. Nor does it matter if the truth was published maliciously; the press is free to sustain a campaign against someone it dislikes, provided that the defamatory allegations are accurate. There is one exception to this. Under section 8 of the Rehabilitation of Offenders Act 1974, the defendant remains free to rely on the defence of justification (or fair comment and privilege) if it has referred to the plaintiff's 'spent' conviction for a criminal offence; in these circumstances, however, the defence of truth will be defeated if the plaintiff shows that the allegation was made maliciously.

There is no need for the defendant to prove the truth of every detail. Under the Defamation Act 1952, section 5, the defence will succeed, even if the accuracy of every charge is not substantiated, provided those allegations do not add to the sting of the allegations which are shown to be true. But it may still be difficult to justify allegations, bearing in mind that the trial may occur some years after the publication and that in the meantime witnesses may have died or disappeared, or their recollections may prove unreliable. The media must also take account of the possibility that the jury may award aggravated damages (see later, p. 22) to provide further compensation for the plaintiff, if it finds that the defendant has wrongly persisted in maintaining the truth of the story.

2. Fair comment on a matter of public interest

This defence is the most useful to the media. They must show first that the comment was made on a matter of public interest. That is relatively straightforward.[10] It is for the judge, not the

---

[10] The leading case is *London Artists Ltd.* v. *Littler* [1969] 2 QB 375, where the Court of Appeal held that the premature closing of a West End play was a matter of public interest.

jury, to determine what topics fall under this heading. They extend well beyond politics to include any matter which the public may legitimately discuss or take an interest in, for example, the management of a football club, the performance of sportsmen and other celebrities, or the quality of a show. However, it is important to distinguish a matter of public interest from a matter which the public finds interesting; the fair comment defence will not apply to discussion of the latter.

Secondly, the defendant must show that the facts on which the comment was based were true. This is obviously an essential requirement, for otherwise it would be all too easy to argue that the allegation was an expression of opinion, rather than one of fact, so that it need not be substantiated. If, for instance, a newspaper suggests that a Cabinet Minister is a liar, it must prove the facts on the basis of which that conclusion is drawn. It need not, however, prove the truth of every underlying fact, provided the comment is shown to be fair by reference to some true facts: see Defamation Act 1952, section 6. Nor need the underlying facts be referred to explicitly in the defamatory article itself.

It will, therefore, be important to establish at the outset whether the defamatory statement amounts to a factual claim about, say, the conduct and attitudes of the plaintiff or an opinion about his character. There is some authority for the view that suggestions of dishonest or corrupt behaviour or motives should be regarded as factual,[11] though perhaps their characterization as fact or comment will depend on the context in which they were made. The case of *Telnikoff* v. *Matusevitch*[12] raised the question whether in making this characterization the jury was only entitled to look at the defamatory statement or whether it was also free to look at an article to which it was a reply. The defendant had written a letter to the *Daily Telegraph*, in which he accused the plaintiff, who had a few days previously written an article for the paper, of racialist, anti-Jewish attitudes. On one view this was a

[11] See *Campbell* v. *Spottiswoode* (1863) 32 LJ QB 185.
[12] [1992] 2 AC 343.

comment on the opinion expressed in the article, but the House of Lords ruled that the jury should only take account of the text of the letter. It then clearly amounted to an allegation of fact, which the writer of the letter made no attempt to justify. Lord Ackner dissenting argued that the majority decision constituted a significant deterrent to the publication of readers' letters and imposed a difficult burden on editors.

The *Telnikoff* case also established that it is unnecessary for the defendant to prove that the comment represented his own honest opinion. What he must show is that it was an opinion which could honestly be expressed; it is immaterial how obstinate or prejudiced it was.[13] So a newspaper would not necessarily be liable if it published a letter expressing in intemperate or vitriolic terms a view, say, on the conduct of a public figure which the editor himself did not share. The adjective 'fair' is really a misnomer. On the other hand, the plaintiff can defeat a fair comment defence (or one of qualified privilege) if he proves express malice. In the leading case of *Horrocks* v. *Lowe*[14] the House of Lords explained that the plaintiff rebuts the defence of qualified privilege if he proves the defendant knew that the allegations are untrue or did not believe them to be true. Alternatively (and of more relevance to the fair comment defence) there is malice if it is shown that the defendant acted predominantly out of spite to the plaintiff or to achieve some personal advantage. In practice it is rare for the plaintiff, particularly in media cases, to attempt to rebut a defence in this way.

3. Absolute and qualified privileges

On a number of occasions a publication will be covered by an absolute or qualified privilege. As the word 'absolute' suggests, the former provides a complete defence; if defamatory allegations are made on an occasion covered by such a privilege, the plaintiff

---

[13] See the direction to the jury of Diplock J in *Silkin* v. *Beaverbrook Newspapers Ltd* [1958] 1 WLR 743.   [14] [1975] AC 135.

will be unable to bring an action for libel, even if the words are untrue or the defendant is motivated by malice. In contrast, qualified privilege may be rebutted by proof of malice. But unlike fair comment the defence is available even if the allegations were untrue and the defendant made them carelessly. (But after a recent decision of the House of Lords it seems there may be liability in certain circumstances for the separate tort of negligent misstatement.[15])

The defence of absolute privilege, with one exception, is of no use to the media. The most famous instance of the privilege protects MPs from liability for anything said or written during the course of Parliamentary proceedings: Bill of Rights 1689, article 9. Witnesses and parties to legal proceedings also enjoy a common law absolute privilege, as do counsel and judges. By the Defamation Act 1996, section 14, there is an absolute privilege for fair and accurate contemporaneous reports of judicial proceedings, and this obviously benefits the press and broadcasters.

But apart from this case the media may only claim a qualified privilege. There are privileges for fair and accurate reports of legislative proceedings anywhere in the world and Parliamentary sketches,[16] and also for reports of legal proceedings, even if they are not contemporaneous with the trial (Defamation Act 1996, Schedule I, Part I[17]). Further, qualified privilege protects the publication of reports of the public meetings and notices of a variety of bodies, companies, and officials: see Defamation Act 1996, Schedule I, Part II. The privileges conferred by Part II of the Schedule are conditional, in that a newspaper, broadcaster, or other publisher has no defence if it has been asked by the plaintiff to publish (or transmit) a reasonable statement to explain or contradict the allegation and has refused to do this: Defamation Act 1996, section 15(2). This provision, albeit indirectly, provides in certain circumstances an opportunity for plaintiffs to

---

[15] See *Spring* v. *Guardian Assurance* [1995] 2 AC 296.
[16] Defamation Act 1996, Sch. I, para. 1; *Cook* v. *Alexander* [1974] QB 279.
[17] Defamation Act 1996, Sch. I, para. 2.

reply to defamatory allegations, though it falls short of the right of reply afforded in many continental European jurisdictions. The privilege established by the 1952 Act did not extend to publishers of books and of periodicals published at intervals of more than thirty-six days, e.g., quarterly reviews. But the recent Defamation Act reformulated the privilege to cover all publications.

However, it is important to note that there is no general fair reporting defence for the media. They would report at their peril any defamatory allegations made, say, by a politician or a trade union official in an interview or at a press conference; the report of such remarks made at a *public meeting* (defined in paragraph 12(2) of Schedule 1 to the Act) may be covered by the Defamation Act 1996, but in other circumstances their report would not be. More importantly, in England there is no general privilege for the media to report matters of interest to the public. This was decided by the Court of Appeal in *Blackshaw* v. *Lord*.[18] The *Daily Telegraph* had inaccurately identified the plaintiff, a former civil servant in the Department of Energy, as associated with some government incompetence which had cost £52 million. The plaintiff's libel action succeeded, since the court refused to recognize a common law privilege of the press to communicate information which it wrongly believed to be accurate. (The journalist had got hold of the plaintiff's name from the Department press officer; but his disclosure made over the telephone was not in the form of a government notice, the reporting of which would constitute a statutory privileged occasion.) The recognition of such a broad privilege would have outflanked the requirement of the fair comment defence that it must be based on true facts.

In this respect English law contrasts sharply with libel law in the United States and now in Australia, where to varying extents the courts have in effect created constitutional defences or privileges to libel actions. In the United States public officials and figures must prove that the allegations were false and that the

---

[18] [1984] QB 1.

defendant (usually, but not necessarily the media) published them maliciously, that is, it knew that the story was untrue or was reckless as to its truth.[19] Other plaintiffs must show the defendant was negligent. In Australia the High Court has held that there must be at least a no-negligence defence to libel actions brought by MPs and election candidates.[20] In both these jurisdictions, therefore, the common law strict liability rule has been held incompatible with the constitutional guarantee of freedom of speech. Moreover, the US courts take the view that to require the publisher to prove to the jury's satisfaction the truth of an allegation against a public official or figure would unduly deter, or chill, freedom of political speech. Fear of the chilling effect of libel law on political discussion was the reason given by Lord Keith in the *Derbyshire* case for precluding actions by public authorities. For the same reason the English courts might at some time be prepared to reconsider the decision in *Blackshaw* v. *Lord* and recognize a privilege to publish information of public interest or importance believed on reasonable grounds to be true. ⇐ imp.

4. Offer of amends

The Defamation Act 1952 provided a defence of offer of amends in cases of unintentional defamation, defined as those cases where the publisher had not intended to refer to the plaintiff or had not known of circumstances under which the material had been understood to refer to him (as in *Hulton* v. *Jones*) or where the publisher had not known of the circumstances under which remarks innocent on their face were defamatory by innuendo. The defence only applied where the defendant had taken reasonable care. In these circumstances, it was a complete defence for the publisher to offer a correction and apology, when either

---

[19] This has been established by a line of Supreme Court cases, following the famous decision in *New York Times* v. *Sullivan*, 376 US 254 (1964). For a discussion of these cases and the reasons for the divergent English and US approaches, see F. Schauer, 'Social Foundations of the Law of Defamation' (1980) 1 *Jo. Media Law and Practice* 3.

[20] *Theophanous* v. *Herald and Weekly Times Ltd* (1994) 68 AJLR 713.

the offer had been accepted and the correction, etc. published, or the offer had been refused but was still on the table.

In practice this defence was hardly ever invoked. The Defamation Act 1996 has now considerably expanded its scope with a view to its greater use by the media; the defence will be available whenever the defendant is prepared to offer to publish a correction or apology. Such an offer will always constitute a defence unless the plaintiff can show that the defendant knew or had reason to believe the allegations were false and defamatory of him. So the defence can now be invoked whenever the defendant has got its facts wrong, as long as the libel was not committed deliberately or recklessly. On the other hand, the defendant making the offer must be prepared on its acceptance by the plaintiff to pay compensation in its fulfilment; compensation will be agreed or assessed by a judge (without a jury). It is only if the offer is not accepted by the plaintiff that it amounts to a complete defence (unless as stated the plaintiff can show knowledge, etc.).

Jurisdiction

London is the libel capital of the world, principally owing to the large sums of damages which are awarded by juries from time to time. The rules governing the courts' jurisdiction are, therefore, important. They require only a brief treatment here, since we are concerned with the impact of libel law on national publications where there is generally no dispute about the matter. (The rules about the jurisdiction of the English and Scottish courts for publication within the United Kingdom are considered later.) The English High Court has jurisdiction to hear an action in respect of any publication which took place within the jurisdiction, that is, which is read, heard, or viewed in England. Under this rule the English courts can, for example, hear an action brought in respect of a US paper which enjoys some circulation in England or a US satellite broadcast received here.[21]

---

[21] The principle was applied, for example, to allow Upjohn Ltd. to sue the *New York Times* (as well as the BBC) in a famous libel case in 1994.

The rules are now modified in the context of the European Union by the Brussels Convention on Jurisdiction and the Enforcement of Judgments in Civil and Commercial Matters, implemented in UK law by the Civil Jurisdiction and Judgments Act 1982. The basic rule is that actions should be brought in the courts of the defendant's state of domicile (irrespective of nationality). But it may also be sued in the courts of the place 'where the harmful event occurred'. Recently the European Court of Justice has held that this means that the plaintiff can sue in either the state where the defendant is domiciled (or established) for the whole loss or in each state where the publication was distributed for the loss flowing from publication in that jurisdiction.[22] As a result the plaintiff, an Englishwoman living in England could sue in respect of an alleged libel in *France Soir*, a newspaper with only a minuscule circulation in the country, but only for the damage to her reputation sustained there.

Conversely, is a plaintiff resident in a foreign country entitled to sue in England for a libel in a paper published in England (or a broadcast transmitted from England)? In these circumstances, the main circulation (or audience) is in this country, but there may also be publication in a foreign country and hence damage to the plaintiff's reputation there. The Brussels Convention rules apply where the two states concerned are members of the European Union, that is, in the case hypothesized in the previous sentence, where an English newspaper is also circulated in, say, France or Germany. The English courts have jurisdiction, as do the French or German courts for damage occurring to the plaintiff's reputation there. When, however, the other country is not a member of the EU, the High Court may apply the principle of *forum non conveniens* to decline jurisdiction, where the relevant factors, for example, the terms of the article and the plaintiff's reputation, establish a much closer connection with another country.[23]

---

[22] *Shevill* v. *Presse Alliance SA* [1995] 2 AC 18.
[23] See *Okaro* v. *Observer*, 10 Apr. 1992 (unreported).

Limitation Period

Under the Limitation Act 1980 libel actions could not be brought more than three years after publication (a contrast with the usual limitation period of six years for tort claims). The reasons for the limitation period are the same as for other types of civil action: witnesses die or their memories fade, and it becomes more difficult to determine the facts. These points apply with particular force to defamation cases, where much may turn on interpretation of the plaintiff's conduct. Delay poses especially grave problems for broadcasters, where the programme is made by an independent producer, perhaps on the basis of research by a freelance journalist: in this context it is very easy to lose notes and records. Application of the limitation period to claims against book publishers also creates difficulties for them, in that a book may be sold, and hence published for purposes of the limitation period, years after its initial issue: see further discussion in Chapter 6.

The Defamation Act 1996 has further reduced the limitation period to one year. But it is recognized that in some exceptional circumstances plaintiffs have a good reason for delay in issuing a writ. For example, initially they may not believe they can meet the costs of bringing an action. A less persuasive reason for tolerating delay is that a plaintiff may prefer to await the outcome of another inquiry before deciding whether it is worth pursuing a libel action; this might be the investigation of a complaint to the Broadcasting Complaints Commission or to the Police Complaints Authority. At all events, the courts have wide discretion in appropriate cases to extend the limitation period beyond the normal limitation period of one year.

The Role of Judge and Jury

Perhaps the most distinctive feature of libel actions in England (but not Scotland) is that generally they are tried by jury. This is very unusual in civil cases. Either party is entitled to request a jury trial, unless it would involve a lengthy examination of documents or scientific investigations which make this course inconvenient. Even then the judge may order trial by jury. The right of the jury to determine whether the words are defamatory dates back to Fox's Libel Act 1792, when libel proceedings were criminal rather than civil. During the nineteenth century this right was regarded as a valuable safeguard for freedom of speech and of the press, so it is a nice irony that now it is the media who are most critical of the jury's role.

It is for the jury to determine the meaning of the allegation, whether it constitutes defamation, and whether any defence has been made out, and most controversially the level of damages. The judge may decide whether an allegation is capable of bearing a particular meaning, and whether that meaning could in law be defamatory. He also rules on what constitutes a matter of public interest for the fair comment defence and whether the publication is covered by qualified privilege.[24] But it is for the jury to determine whether on the facts the defence succeeds.

In the last few years some famous cases have been heard by a judge sitting without a jury, for example, the action by Upjohns against the BBC and the *New York Times,* and also the epic litigation conducted by McDonalds to preserve their reputation for the provision of fast but edible food. Moreover, the Faulks Committee argued for removing the assessment of damages from the jury; it should determine liability, but the judge should determine the quantum of damages.[25] But jury trial on both questions is still the norm.

Two recent developments affect the role of the jury. The first is potentially the most important reform achieved by the Defamation Act 1996. Under section 8, the judge may decide in some circumstances to dispose of a defamation case summarily, that is,

---

[24] But the Court of Appeal has ruled that what constitutes 'a matter of public concern' for the availability of the qualified privileges provided by the Defamation Act 1952 is for the jury: *Kingshott* v. *Associated Kent Newspapers* [1991] 1 QB 88. The point is not affected by the 1996 Bill.

[25] (1975) Cmnd. 5909, para. 454.

without a jury trial. For instance, he may dismiss the plaintiff's case if it is hopeless, or give her summary relief if the defence has no 'realistic prospect of success' and such relief would provide her with adequate compensation. But the judge can only award up to £10,000 under this procedure, and it is possible that this ceiling (which may be raised by the Lord Chancellor) is too low to encourage frequent use of the procedure.

The second development relates to judicial control over jury awards of damages. Until recently the judge could only give the jury general guidance on the level of damages. In particular, he could not refer it to damages awards in previous libel cases or in other civil litigation, for example, personal injuries cases. At the end of 1995 the Court of Appeal substantially revised the law in this area: a jury could be referred to awards in personal injuries cases as a check on the reasonableness of the sum it had in mind, and it would induce realism to allow counsel and the judge to mention appropriate figures.[26] The Court also affirmed its own earlier decision that it would be appropriate to refer the jury to the awards it now makes under its new power to assess damages on appeal (see further p. 24).[27] On the other hand, *at present* juries should not be reminded of previous jury awards in libel cases, on the ground that, as they were (most likely) made without guidance from the judge, they would be unreliable markers.

Remedies

Under this heading we consider the availability of injunctions and the heads and level of damages which may be awarded for libel. It is worth pointing out that the range of *legally enforceable remedies* is relatively narrow, compared, for example, to those available in

---

[26] *Elton John* v. *MGN* [1996] 2 All ER 35. The Law Commission has recommended that libel juries should be referred to the range of awards for non-pecuniary loss in personal injuries cases: see *Damages for Personal Injury: Non-Pecuniary Loss* (1995) Consultation Paper No. 140.

[27] *Rantzen* v. *Mirror Group Newspapers Ltd* [1994] QB 670.

other European legal systems. There is no enforceable right of reply as such, though the media may have a comparable duty to publish a letter or statement by way of explanation or contradiction as a condition of the statutory qualified privilege (see above, p. 13). Nor is there a right to have a false statement retracted, though an apology may be published in fulfilment of an offer of amends: see above, p. 16.

1. Injunctions

The courts are very reluctant to grant an interlocutory injunction to restrain the further publication of an alleged libel before full trial. Under what is generally known as the rule in *Bonnard* v. *Perryman*,[28] they will not do this when the defendant intends to justify or to argue fair comment or privilege. Otherwise the law would in effect impose a prior restraint on a publication which is true or made on a privileged occasion.[29] There is, however, no difficulty in obtaining the grant of am injunction against a publisher whose defence at trial has failed.

2. Damages

As already mentioned, it is for the jury to determine the amount of damages. In English law they can be divided into two heads: *compensatory* and *exemplary*. Compensatory damages may be further sub-divided into general and special damages. The latter is in most cases less important and easier to explain. They compensate the plaintiff for any special loss flowing from the libel, which can be measured in pecuniary terms. An obvious example would be the loss of particular contracts as a consequence of damage to commercial reputation. (In contrast, an unquantifiable loss of business would fall under general damages.)

---

[28] [1891] 2 Ch. 269.
[29] See the judgement of Lord Denning MR in *Fraser* v. *Evans* [1969] 1 QB 349, 360.

The purpose of general damages is in the first place to vindicate the plaintiff's reputation, that is, to show to the world that the defamatory charge was groundless. They also provide compensation for his injured feelings and other losses which cannot be reduced to pecuniary terms. Juries obviously consider that sums such as the £500,000 awarded to Jeffrey Archer (as he then was) in 1987 or the £750,000 awarded to Graham Souness in 1995 are justified to achieve these ends. While these figures are unusually high, six figure awards are not uncommon.

Additional compensatory damages may be awarded where the plaintiff's feelings have been further injured by the defendant's behaviour, either at or subsequent to publication. These *aggravated* damages, as they are known, may be awarded, for example, for the gratuitous repetition of the libel, for persistence in maintaining a groundless plea of justification, or for hostile cross-examination of the plaintiff. Although they appear to 'punish' the defendant, they can only be awarded to compensate the plaintiff for the injury presumed to flow from this behaviour and they should not be confused with *exemplary* or *punitive* damages, discussed later in this section.

Conversely, damages may be reduced if the plaintiff does not enjoy a good reputation. The purpose of a libel action is to protect the reputation to which the plaintiff is entitled, not one to which he is not entitled. But there have been strict limits on the evidence which may be adduced to show that the plaintiff does not have a good reputation. While general evidence of bad reputation is admissible, under the rule in *Scott* v. *Sampson*[30] evidence of particular misconduct not covered by a plea of justification is inadmissible. (The Neill Committee on Practice and Procedure in Defamation recommended abolition of the rule to enable evidence to be given of specific misconduct which relates to the same sector of the plaintiff's life as the alleged libel; a provision to give effect

---

[30] (1882) 8 QBD 491. But under what is said to be an exception to the rule evidence of previous convictions may be given: *Goody* v. *Odhams Press* [1967] 1 QB 333.

to this proposal was incorporated in the Defamation Bill 1996, but was removed at a late stage during its passage through the Commons.)

The other head is exemplary damages. Sometimes described as 'punitive' damages, there are strict limits on the circumstances on which they may be awarded in tort actions.[31] In the context of libel it is only appropriate to award them when the defendant knew the publication was defamatory and could not be justified, or was reckless as to these matters, and calculated that any gain to be made from publication exceeded the compensation payable.[32] The restrictiveness of this formula may explain why it is relatively uncommon for such awards to be made; another explanation, of course, might be that the high level of compensatory damages means that plaintiffs need not generally claim under this other head.[33]

The availability of exemplary damages in libel, as in some other contexts, has long been a matter of controversy. On one view it is wrong in principle to punish the defendant in civil proceedings and give a windfall to the plaintiff; on the other hand, it is argued they are necessary to deter the media, in particular the national tabloids, from committing deliberate defamation, where publication of the story will boost circulation. The Neill Committee recommended the abolition of exemplary damages. However, the Law Commission's provisional view is that they still have a place. The conditions for their award should be reformed, so that they are available only when the parties are in an unequal relationship and the publisher has shown a disregard for the plaintiff's personality rights.

Until recently the Court of Appeal had little power to interfere with a jury's damages award. In the absence of any misdirection

---

[31] The circumstances in which it is appropriate to award these damages are set out in Lord Devlin's speech in *Rookes* v. *Barnard* [1964] AC 1129, 1226, and see now *Elton John* v. *MGN* [1996] 2 All ER 35, 55–8.

[32] See *Broome* v. *Cassell* [1972] AC 1027.

[33] See Law Commission Consultation Paper No. 132, *Aggravated, Exemplary and Restitutionary Damages*, paras. 3.44–3.51.

by the judge, it would allow an appeal only if the award was one
that no reasonable jury could have made. Moreover, it could not
itself reassess the damages unless the parties agreed to this course,
but had to order a new trial on the issue. However, under section
8 of the Courts and Legal Services Act 1990 discretion was
conferred on the Court of Appeal to award the damages it thinks
appropriate instead of ordering a new trial whenever it considers
the jury award excessive or inadequate. This power was exercised
to reduce an award of £250,000 to Esther Rantzen to one of
£110,000, on the ground that the jury award was disproportionate
to the injury suffered by the plaintiff.[34] The Court of Appeal held
it should take into account Article 10 of the European Human
Rights Convention in using its new power to revise excessive
awards. In this context, it is interesting to note that in 1995 the
European Court of Human Rights upheld the Commission
decision that the record award of £1,500,000 to Lord Aldington
could not be regarded as a restriction on freedom of expression,
which was necessary and proportionate to safeguard the right to
reputation.[35]

It is the unpredictability of jury awards, perhaps more than any
other factor, which makes the outcome of libel trials such a
lottery. It also makes more of a gamble the defendant's decision
how much to pay into court and the plaintiff's decision whether to
accept such a payment. Under the Rules of Court a payment made
by the defendant into court at any stage after entry of an
appearance in the action may be accepted by the plaintiff up to
twenty-one days after this payment.[36] Acceptance ends the
proceedings. If the plaintiff, however, does not accept this
payment and is awarded damages lower than that amount, he will
not be entitled to reimbursement from the losing defendant of his
costs incurred after the date of payment.[37] The jury, of course,
does not know whether, and what sort of, payment has been

---

[34] *Rantzen* v. *Mirror Group Newspapers (1986) Ltd* [1994] QB 670.
[35] *Tolstoy* v. *UK* (1995) 20 EHRR 442.   [36] RSC, Ord. 22.
[37] *Ibid.*, Ord. 62, r. 5.

made. So a newspaper aware that it will have difficulty in defending a libel action may make a payment into court, hoping the plaintiff will accept in the belief she is unlikely to win more damages. Both parties will engage in the hopeless task of guessing what the jury may award.

The Law in Scotland

While the general principles, and most of the rules, of defamation law are the same in Scotland as in England, there are a number of significant differences, both in the rules themselves and in the philosophy behind the law. The practical effect that these differences have will be explored in rather more depth in Chapter 8, but the following paragraphs will identify the major areas in which the rules of Scots defamation law vary from those of English law as described earlier in this Chapter.

As was pointed out above, there is no formal distinction in Scots law between libel and slander: defamation is the communication of a false and derogatory idea and the method of communication is irrelevant. The major distinction in Scotland is between defamation and what is today referred to as 'verbal injury' (the English equivalent being malicious falsehood). Also, there is no need to prove 'publication' in the technical English sense: there must be communication but that can be to the pursuer alone. This is a consequence of the fact that defamation in Scotland is designed primarily to assuage hurt feelings rather than to vindicate public reputation. Defamation in Scotland is a purely civil wrong and there is today no crime of defamation.[38]

As far as the definition of a defamatory statement is concerned Lord Atkin's test in *Sim* v. *Stretch* has been accepted by the Scottish courts.[39] Though the level of claims is much lower in

---

[38] Criminal defamation did exist in previous centuries but it withered in the early years of the 19th century, and there is no possibility of the High Court of Justiciary reviving defamation as a crime.

[39] See *Steele* v. *Scottish Daily Record and Sunday Mail*, 1970 SLT 53.

Scotland, the profile of pursuers is remarkably similar and there is little variation in the rules concerning entitlement to sue. One difference that does exist concerns defamatory statements relating to dead persons. The English rule[40] is that the death of either plaintiff or defendant brings any action to an end and prevents any action being raised thereafter. In Scotland, on the other hand, an executor can continue an action raised before death by a pursuer and recover both patrimonial loss (economic loss) and solatium (general damages for hurt feelings); and an executor can raise an action after death which the defamed person had not raised before death, but can recover only patrimonial loss to the estate.[41] It has been argued[42] that an executor can raise an action based on verbal injury for harmful statements made about a deceased person after his death, though there is no judicial authority supporting that proposition.

The defences described above in English law exist in Scotland, though often they are less well developed. This is particularly so, for example, with 'innocent dissemination', which had never in those terms been accepted as a defence in Scots law, though there was little doubt that it, or something similar, applied in Scotland. The reformulated defence set out in the Defamation Act 1996 applies to Scots law, as does the revision of the offer-of-amends defence. The defence of 'justification' applies in Scotland, where it is known as '*veritas*', or truth. Part of the definition of a defamatory statement is that it is false (though *veritas* has the effect of a defence since Scots law, as does English law, presumes a derogatory statement to be false). In England it is justifiable to tell the truth about someone; in Scotland it may or may not be justifiable, but it is not defamation. Fair comment applies in Scotland, though with this difference: there is no Scottish

---

[40] Law Reform (Miscellaneous Provisions) Act 1934, s. 1(1).

[41] Damages (Scotland) Act 1976, s. 2(4), as substituted by the Damages (Scotland) Act 1993.

[42] Norrie, *Defamation and Related Actions in Scots Law* (Butterworths, Edinburgh, 1995) at 57–60 and 73–4.

authority to suggest that to be fair the comment must be made honestly, or in a belief that it is justified. In Scotland the defence can be made out, so long as the comment is a comment rather than a statement of fact and so long as it is a relevant comment on a fact.[43] The period of limitation in Scotland is three years, which can be extended in exceptional circumstances.[44] The reduction made by the Defamation Act 1996 in the general limitation period to one year does not apply to Scottish actions.

Privileges, qualified and absolute, apply in Scotland as in England, though the categories of statement that fall into each form of privilege are sometimes different. The Law of Libel Amendment Act 1888 did not apply in Scotland, but the Defamation Act 1952 and relevant provisions of the 1996 legislation do. Thus fair and accurate contemporaneous reports of court proceedings enjoy absolute privilege, while other reports enjoy qualified privilege as in England. Within court proceedings, though most of the participants, such as judge, jury, counsel, witnesses, are protected by absolute privilege, in Scotland the parties to civil proceedings are protected only by qualified privilege.

Defamation actions are raised in the Court of Session, though it is not unknown for them to be raised in the Sheriff Court which enjoys competence to hear them. Civil juries were abolished in the latter in 1980, but it is still possible for a jury to sit in the Court of Session. Though the legislation in the two jurisdictions governing when jury trial is permitted is very similar, in practice juries are very rare in Scotland. The courts in defamation action still talk, however, of 'jury questions' when they mean questions of fact.

The most immediately noticeable difference between the Scots and English law of defamation concerns the remedies available. Interdict is available in Scotland as injunction is (sometimes) in England, though the Scottish courts are noticeably less reluctant

---

[43] *Ibid.*, 147–9.
[44] Prescription and Limitation (Scotland) Act 1973, ss. 7, 18A, 19A and Sch. 1, para. 2(gg).

than their counterparts south of the border to grant this remedy: the pursuer need show only a *prima facie* case of defamation and that the granting of an interim interdict satisfies the balance of convenience.[45] The normal remedy is damages, and assessment of damages is on very different principles in Scotland. Damages in Scots law (and not just in relation to defamation) are designed solely to compensate for loss, and it follows that exemplary or punitive damages are anathema to Scots law and are never in any circumstances awarded. Damages are of two kinds: pecuniary damages which compensate for the precise economic loss that the pursuer can show as resulting from the defamation, and solatium, or a monetary solace for the pursuer's hurt feelings at the loss of his reputation. Solatium of its nature can never be assessed precisely and is similar to the English notion of general damages, but the level of assessment is very much lower in Scotland than in England. This matter is explored more fully in Chapter 8 below.

The Inner House of the Court of Session (the appeal court) has no power similar to the English Court of Appeal's power to substitute its own award for an award made in a lower court by a judge or jury; it may, however, order a new trial limited to the amount of damages if it considers the original assessment to be unreasonably high or unreasonably low.

Legal aid is available in Scotland for neither defamation nor verbal injury (while in England legal aid is available for malicious falsehood).

Jurisdiction in England and Scotland

Jurisdiction is governed by the Civil Jurisdiction and Judgments Act 1982, which provides that actions for damages can be raised in the courts of the 'domicile' of the defender. 'Domicile' is defined to mean the country in which the defender is resident and has a substantive connection with. If the defender is a corporation or association then its domicile is where it has its 'seat', that is the

---

[45] See Norrie, n. 42 above, 175–6.

country *either* (a) under the law of which it was incorporated or formed and where it has its registered office or some other official address, *or* (b) where its central management and control are exercised.[46] Media defenders are normally corporations and it follows that an action against them can be raised where the corporation has its seat, as defined. This gives pursuers and plaintiffs a fairly free hand within the United Kingdom, for most national media outlets in Scotland will have offices in England giving jurisdiction to the English courts, and all the national media based in England publish to some extent in Scotland. Some newspaper organizations in Scotland have suggested that they are sometimes sued in England when the natural forum would be the Scottish court, but there is no evidence to suggest that this occurs with great frequency. Applying the rule in the *France Soir* case mentioned earlier in this chapter would allow most Scottish pursuers to raise their actions in England, but mostly they choose not to do so. Any attraction England has to offer in the shape of larger awards of damages may well be counterbalanced by the fact that the costs of raising the action there are significantly higher than the costs in Scotland, where there is no specialist defamation bar.

There is currently confusion as to the English courts' power to dismiss an action by a Scottish plaintiff on a plea of *forum non conveniens*. As was mentioned earlier, this plea is not available between Member States of the European Union, but neither Scotland nor England is a Member State (they are both constituent parts of a Member State). In one case, involving an alleged defamatory statement in the Edinburgh-published *Scotland on Sunday*, the plaintiff sued in England notwithstanding that less than 10 per cent of the paper's circulation was within that jurisdiction, and the judge held that he was unable to dismiss the action on a plea of *forum non conveniens*.[47] However, in another

---

[46] Civil Jurisdiction and Judgments Act 1982, s. 42.
[47] *Foxen* v. *Scotsman Publications Ltd*, 1995 EMLR 145; *The Times*, 17 Feb. 1994.

case (decided, curiously, by the same judge) the plaintiff sued in England the Glasgow-published *Scottish Daily Record* which again has less than 10 per cent of its circulation in England; this time the plea of *forum non conveniens* was upheld and the action in the English court dismissed.[48] If the Court of Appeal resolves this dispute by following the latter decision, Scottish media defenders will feel protected from what is widely perceived as an iniquity. Whether their practices and policies in relation to defamation law in general would be altered will be explored in Chapter 8 below.

---

[48] *Cummings* v. *Scottish Daily Record and Sunday Mail*, 1995 EMLR 538; *The Times*, 8 June 1995.

2

Research on the Impact of Libel Law

Introduction

This Chapter outlines in general terms the objects of our research and our research methods. It also presents our findings on the incidence of libel actions against the media, drawn from research on the numbers of cases set down for trial in the Royal Courts of Justice. Some other statistical information taken from the annual *Judicial Statistics* issued by the Lord Chancellor's Department is summarized.

It should be stated at the outset that our research provides only a partial insight into the operation of this area of the law. It was designed in the first place to study the impact of defamation law on the media, in particular the principal mass media of the press and broadcasting. We did not examine the attitudes of libel plaintiffs nor determine the difficulties they face in bringing or maintaining a libel action in the courts. However, we did interview some lawyers who work entirely or mainly for libel plaintiffs, largely to build a more complete picture by obtaining another perspective on the concerns expressed by the media and their lawyers. Nor was it possible with the resources available to obtain figures on the number of libel writs taken out against the media in general or particular branches of the media in contrast with the global figures for all libel writs published since 1992 in *Judicial Statistics*. We were advised that it would take a team of researchers several months to examine all the libel writs issued in the Royal Courts of Justice in order to categorize them by libel defendant. Finally, and most importantly, we would like to emphasize that the figures in the second half of this Chapter do not represent the real impact of libel law on the daily activities of journalists and media lawyers. The greatest impact of the law occurs before publication or transmission when the media and their advisers are concerned to avoid legal difficulties; moreover, only a small proportion of complaints are followed by a writ (a matter taken up in later chapters), and most writs do not lead to a full trial or even to the case being set down for trial.

Research Objects

The object of our research, as stated in our application to the Economic and Social Research Council for financial support, was to assess the impact of defamation law on the media, especially the press and broadcasting media. The background to the research was the concern frequently expressed by editors, journalists, and broadcasters, as well as by their legal represent- atives, that the law of libel constitutes a significant fetter on their freedom of expression to publish stories of real public interest. They argue that some of the rules discussed in the first chapter of this book, in particular the presumption of falsity and the consequent burden on the defendant to prove truth or show fair comment, mean that they are unwilling to publish stories which they believe on good evidence to be accurate. Other factors deterring publication are, the media claim, the high cost of defending libel actions, and the large damage awards which may be made by juries. As we have seen (see p. 15 above) the US Supreme Court, and more recently the High Court of Australia, have accepted that libel law does exercise a 'chilling effect' on the freedom of the press and broadcasting media. More pertinently, the House of Lords took the same view when it held that public authorities were not entitled to protect their reputation by bringing defamation proceedings (see p. 6 above).

So one aim of our research was to assess so far as possible whether, and how far, the rules of defamation law do deter the publication of stories of real public interest. But that was only one of our objectives. We also wanted to present a comprehensive picture of the impact of this area of law on the daily work of editors, journalists, producers, and their lawyers. This involved answering a number of questions. Do concerns about the potential impact of a libel action, or dealing with an actual claim, take up much time? How many lawyers did each newspaper or broadcaster employ, and how often do the media go to an outside solicitor or counsel for advice before deciding whether to publish or broadcast an item? What are the procedures for dealing with complaints, and in this and other contexts what are the relationships between journalist and editors on the one hand, and their legal advisers on the other? We were also concerned to find out what sorts of items were most frequently suppressed or amended before publication or transmission: how far were they items about politicians, the City, sports personalities, or pop stars? And as far as the broadcasting media were concerned, which types of programme were most affected: news and current affairs, documentaries, docu-drama, or soap opera? Finally, we wanted to obtain an impression of how much libel costs in terms of annual payments for damages, legal costs, insurance premiums, and so on.

Initially, we had decided to concentrate on the mass media, that is the press and broadcasting. But we became convinced that we should also investigate the impact of defamation law on the publication of books and periodicals, where some economic and others factors might operate in a particular way which differentiated their position from that of the mass media. For example, the costs of withdrawing a book or magazine from the shelves after the threat of a legal action might make their publishers particularly careful of libel risks. On the other hand, some magazines such as *Private Eye* and *Scallywag* have thrived on publishing stories which, they claim, national newspapers and broadcasting channels have been frightened, for legal reasons, to publish, and it was clearly interesting to investigate why this was apparently the case.

One other general point is worth making. The research was largely conceived in legal terms: what is the impact of the present rules of libel law on the media? But it was also intended to be, and certainly became, a study of sociological interest. In the first place, our research revealed a lot of information about the relationships of different players in what may be termed the libel game. In particular, we heard much about relationships within organizations, for example, national newspapers, the BBC, and commercial channels, especially between journalists, editors, and their in-house legal advisers. We were also concerned with the relationships between independent actors, such as those between authors and publishers and between independent producers and broadcasting companies. These are in principle governed by contract. But we found that other considerations sometimes affect the relationship, for example, the friendship which may develop over a period of years between authors and publishers.

We also investigated the extent to which the media took into account the characteristics of the person or institution which might launch proceedings if a possibly defamatory article were published or item broadcast. How much attention was paid, for instance, to his propensity to sue and his record against that particular company or against other branches of the media? Were they more prepared to take risks if the subject of the article was unlikely to sue, or unable to finance legal proceedings? How important was the calculation that he or she would be funded by a professional body or attract the support of a financial backer? We wondered how important these factors are in practice, and how they relate to the more obviously legal questions whether the item is defamatory and, if so, whether it could be defended success-fully in court.

We should emphasize at this point that it was not our object to construct a case for reform of the libel laws. Given the limited nature of our research, that would have been too ambitious. It may be that our research does reveal and highlight some issues which should be put on the law reform agenda, a matter we return to at the end of the concluding chapter. That, however, was not its object. We aimed simply to investigate the impact of the law on the media, and it is not for us to judge whether our findings significantly strengthen the case for reform.

Research Methods

Broadly we used two principal means to acquire information. In the first place we addressed questionnaires to editors and lawyers. (The questions and answers in each questionnaire are reproduced or summarized in the particular chapters dealing with the various branches of the media.) These questionnaires were either addressed by us to individual lawyers or editors, or sent out on our behalf as a mass mailing by representative organizations. Secondly, we conducted interviews with various journalists, editors, producers, and lawyers working for newspapers, broadcasters, and other media publishers. As already mentioned, we also interviewed solicitors who represented plaintiffs as well as media, and other, defendants in libel actions. Many of these were one-off interviews at which a wide range of questions were asked, to some extent supplementing matters covered by the questionnaires.

We also conducted series of interviews, generally four in number spread over a period of two or three months, with lawyers working for some of the national newspapers and some of the larger broadcasting companies. The object of these repeated interviews was to establish the pattern of libel work coming through the lawyers' offices and to reduce the risk that an isolated interview would take place after an unusually light or heavy period of work and so give us a distorted impression. We asked the lawyer concerned to make a note of his activity during the period of two or three weeks between interviews to enable him/her to give us a comprehensive picture of his work.

As this account suggests, most of the interviews were conducted with lawyers. This was particularly the case with the national newspapers and the major broadcasting organizations, many of which (as will be seen in later chapters) employ in-house legal staff to deal with libel and other matters of media law, though some prefer to rely on solicitors outside. We conjectured, rightly, that all major libel matter, whether before or after publication or transmission, ends up, as it were, on their desks—although of course journalists, and in some instances editors and others, are also involved. But the lawyers frequently referred us to journalists, producers, editors, and others to explore other angles. We interviewed them and are satisfied that we have obtained a complete picture of how libel impacts on the different people working in each media organization.

In another respect, however, our account is less full than we would have wished. We found some institutions were ready to give us general information about the financial costs and impact of libel on their operations. This was true of regional newspapers, and to a lesser extent broadcasters. However, national news-papers were for the most part unwilling to give us helpful information on this matter. It should be added that it was more difficult to obtain statistical and other information from them than it proved to be from regional papers, broadcasters, and other branches of the media. That is perhaps partly attributable to the intense pressure of work under which national newspapers operate. Another explanation is that they feel this information is sufficiently sensitive to be exploited by potential litigants and so weaken their position with regard to their competitors. Moreover, the Associated Newspapers group refused to grant us regular interviews for reasons of this character. That was however an isolated case.

Of course, some information was given to us on the under-standing that names, factual details, and figures should not be quoted, or not quoted in conjunction with the identity of the informant or the company for which he or she worked. We have respected these understandings and are satisfied that we have not broken any confidence in reproducing the information provided in the rest of this book. In any case, the law of libel imposes constraints on us, as well as on our informants. But we are satisfied that, although on occasion some colour may be missing from our account, the following chapters give an accurate picture of the impact of defamation law on the media.

Defamation Writs

Since 1992 the Lord Chancellor's Department has published the number of defamation writs taken out in the Royal Courts of Justice in London. The figures for the years 1992–5 are as follows:

1992	337 writs
1993	336 writs
1994	418 writs
1995	560 writs

The figure of 418 defamation writs in 1994 (Table 3.2 of *Judicial Statistics* 1994, Cm. 2891) compares with 1,474 for personal injuries writs and 299 for other negligence writs. An interesting comparison in the field of media law is that there were in the same year 244 Chancery Division writs for passing-off and trade mark actions and 1,058 for alleged copyright and design right infringements. The increase in the number of writs in 1995 is quite striking, and seems to indicate that libel is a growth industry.

Interesting though these figures are, they do not tell us exactly how many libel writs are issued annually against the media. For a start, they do not distinguish between libel and slander cases, though it is a very safe surmise that the overwhelming majority of writs are for the former and so might implicate the media. But not all libel actions involve the media. As the *Tolstoy* and more recently the *McDonalds* cases indicate, libel actions can be taken against the writers and distributors of leaflets. Another point is that writs can be taken out in any of the numerous District Registries; their number is not recorded in *Judicial Statistics*, but is thought to be small compared to the number of writs taken out in London.

Cases Set Down for Trial in the Royal Courts of Justice

The following information was taken from the records of the High Court in the Royal Courts of Justice in London. Our principal source was the register that records, and charts the progress of, writs set down for trial. It should be stated that the figures taken from the register are approximate for two reasons. First, the register is compiled for internal use and is not designed for statistical purposes. Entries are not always made in a consistent manner or in a way which is easy to interpret. Secondly, the process of extracting information from it is not an exact one. It involved initially the identification of media defendants in libel cases by isolating the defendant newspapers, broadcasters, publishers, etc. named in writs which had been set down for trial by jury. In addition, some writs issued against individual defendants in jury allocated cases were examined; the reason is that often plaintiffs sue the journalist/programme-maker/editor individually rather than the media organization. In these circumstances it is impossible to identify the media cases directly from the register, and it is often necessary to examine the particular writ to determine whether the case is a libel one or another type of action which may be set down for trial by jury, e.g., an action for malicious prosecution. However, it would take a great deal of time for even a large research team to go through all the hundreds of thousands of writs issued from 1990–4, so except for 1994 only a sample of writs were examined. This means that inevitably our figures may not be absolutely exact.

A further complication is that a libel writ may be listed in the register as a non-jury case and thus escape detection during the search process described in the previous paragraph. A writ may be listed as a non-jury case when the parties to the action have settled but they want nevertheless a statement read in open court. In order to incorporate as many of these instances as possible into our figures, writs against media organizations or individuals were examined, irrespective of whether they were listed for a jury trial or not.

Although the figures in the Tables set out below may therefore not be absolutely precise, we believe they give a reliable indication of the scale of libel work which is done in the Royal Courts of Justice.

Table 1. *Libel writs set down for trial*

	1990	1991	1992	1993	1994
Libel Writs set down for trial	87	37	54	47	64
Media Libel Writs set down for trial	63	31	34	24	52

Table 2. *Breakdown of media writs set down for trial*

	1990	1991	1992	1993	1994
Broadcasters	3	5	8	4	7
National Newspapers	45	19	20	15	25
Regional/Local Newspapers	7	1	5	1	4
Periodicals	6	4	1	3	12
Book Publishers	3	2	–	1	4

Notes:
1. In 1990 the breakdown includes one writ that had two media defendants.
2. In 1991 the breakdown includes one writ that had a media plaintiff and defendant.

Table 3. *Outcome of media writs set down for trial*

	1990	1991	1992	1993	1994
Judgment for Plaintiff	1	3	2	2	1
Judgment for Defendant	1	–	–	2	1
Settled or withdrawn	45	22	27	17	28
No action recorded	16	6	5	3	23

Notes:
1. 'No action recorded' indicates that there was no entry in the Register as to the outcome of the Writ.
2. 'Settled or withdrawn' indicates that the writ has been taken out of the litigation process at some time after being set down for trial. It includes writs where the case was settled prior to trial and at trial.

The first point to emerge from these Tables is that only a small proportion of libel writs lead to the case being set down for trial, let alone to a trial itself. It would be very difficult to calculate the exact proportion, since the cases set down for trial in, say, 1994, would overwhelmingly be of actions initiated by a writ served in an earlier year, sometimes a much earlier year. The most that can be said from a comparison of the figures taken from *Judicial Statistics* with the records of cases set down for trial is that at most about one in ten libel action gets as far as that stage.

However, it is very clear from Table 2 that national newspapers represent the vast majority of media defendants in libel writs set down for trial. Within this group, analysis of the litigants involved shows that there are a number of repeat players in the litigation process. For example, in 1990, one national newspaper, the Mirror Group, with ten writs, was a defendant in 22 per cent of all national newspaper cases and 15 per cent of media cases set down for trial. A second newspaper group, News International, with five newspaper titles (*The Times, Sunday Times, Sun, Today, News of the World*) had fourteen cases, that is 31 per cent of the national newspaper libel cases set down for trial and 22 per cent of the media cases. In 1991, the same defendants' shares were Mirror Group, seven cases, 36 per cent/22 per cent, and Newsgroup/Newspaper Publishing eight cases, 42 per cent/25 per cent respectively. In contrast, some national papers had few, if any cases, which got to this stage. Among them are the *Financial Times* and the papers in the Telegraph group.

The samples from the other media sectors are too small to warrant much comment. The BBC and Channel 4 were the only broadcasting companies involved in more than five cases set down for trial. As far as periodicals are concerned, the publisher of *Private Eye*, Pressdram, was involved in half the periodical libel cases set down for trial in 1990, nearly all of them in 1991 and 1992, and a third in 1993. However, in 1994 it was the defendant in only one of the twelve periodicals cases set down for trial in London that year. Again, we would want to conclude with the observation that the low number of writs taken out against a particular media outlet, let alone one particular publisher, says nothing about the importance of this area of law for that branch of the media. Cases in court and writs represent only the tip of a very large iceberg.

3

National Newspapers

Introduction

When we first approached a cross-section of national newspapers in 1991, explaining that we intended to conduct an empirical study of the way in which libel law and practice conditioned their conduct and performance, we received a gratifyingly positive reaction. There seemed to be a general initial agreement that the libel regime as a whole, in any case so far as England and Wales were concerned, was unsatisfactory. There was even perhaps a surprising willingness to discuss individual cases involving libel. With the sole exception of the Associated Newspapers Group (the *Daily Mail, Mail on Sunday,* and *Evening Standard*), all the editors and company executives we approached gave our proposed research project their blessing and gave us permission to talk directly to journalists on their papers, to in-house legal advisers and, where this applied, to the outside firms of solicitors which handle their libel matters. The only universal reservation from the start was that they would not be prepared for us to be given information about aspects of past or pending libel litigation, or threats of litigation, that might indicate a pattern in the tactics they deployed towards particular complaints or classes of complaint. The reason given was that the world of libel litigation in London is a small one, dominated by a handful of firms of solicitors who have made a speciality of it, and by an even smaller number of specialist barristers, belonging to two or at the most three sets of chambers. Widespread awareness of an individual newspaper's tactics, therefore, might quickly prove commercially damaging. Accordingly, we gave a general undertaking that, in what we came to write, no individual newspaper would be identified with the handling of a particular libel case.

Our original intention was to supply a cross-section of newspaper executives or the appropriate in-house legal adviser(s) with a detailed questionnaire designed to elucidate basic facts about national newspapers and defamation: the volume and nature of libel or libel-related complaints from readers; the staff and financial resources and the time directly attributable to handling libel; the reasons why particular courses of action were advised and/or taken before publication; the ways in which post-publication complaints about defamatory or allegedly defamatory matter were handled and the reasons for these decisions; and the extent to which libel practice was perceived as inhibiting or preventing the publication of material considered to be true and worthy of publication: i.e. how far did libel law and practice exercise a 'chilling factor' preventing the printing of material of public interest. We then proposed to use the replies to these questionnaires as the basis for a series of regular short interviews over a period of time with the appropriate newspaper executive in order to cross-check the evidence provided by questionnaire against a newspaper's actual libel experience over a period of months.

In practice we found our interlocutors on the individual newspapers either unable or unwilling to fill out the basic questionnaires. In part, for the reason mentioned above, there was a reluctance to put down in writing for us figures on how much an individual title spent over a typical period on solicitors' and barristers fees on its own account and on damages and costs to complainants or, where actual proceedings had been set in train, to plaintiffs. The main reason, however, for our failure to acquire anything like a comprehensive set of questionnaire returns was that those who might have filled them in for us did not have the time or resources to do so. Typically one, or at the most two, people are the focus of libel and all the other legal problems— contempt of court, breach of confidence, contract—with which a newspaper deals. In some cases these are in-house lawyers; in other cases they are senior journalists. We rapidly understood that these people did not have the time, in effect, to do basic research within their institutions on our behalf. In every other respect, however, they could as a group not have been more co-operative and generous with their time, and we are accordingly grateful to them.

As a result our principal research method for exploring libel and the national newspaper industry became instead a series of structured interviews with the person responsible for libel complaints on each paper. These interviews followed in general the structure of the originally intended questionnaires, with our questions grouped under the following heads: the number of libel writs; the volume of court work; the outcomes of proceedings; the terms on which complaints/actions were settled; the volume and nature of letters before action and other threats/complaints related to libel; the nature of internal arrangements for handling libel issues; the extent to which articles of public interest are killed or substantially amended before publication; the predominant reasons for deciding not to publish or for making substantial amendments to articles before publication; the areas of newspaper coverage perceived as carrying with them the greatest libel problems; the libel insurance arrangements and their impact on editorial decisions; and the budgetary and financial issues related to libel.

In a number of cases we returned several times within an interval of a few weeks to conduct shorter interviews with the same person in order to cross-check the description given by the first interview of the volume and nature of 'libel business' involving a particular title. In addition, with selected newspapers we conducted interviews with the same basic structure with some editors, managing editors, writing journalists working in 'high risk' areas from the point of view of libel, and solicitors working for firms engaged by individual newspapers to give them advice on libel. Our interviews, conducted during 1994 and 1995, covered nine dailies (four broadsheets, four popular tabloids, and one mid-market tabloid); one specialist paper; and six Sunday papers (two broadsheets, one mid-market tabloid, and three popular tabloids).[1] Given the range and volume of these interviews, we are confident that our failure to receive answers to the detailed questionnaires as originally intended has not materially affected the validity of our findings or conclusions.

Statistical Information

The number of writs issued against national newspapers, as might be expected, varies greatly and is directly related to their editorial character. Among the daily papers, the popular tabloids receive more writs than the others. With the tabloid dailies the extra exposure to litigation clearly derives from the fact that their agendas are significantly more involved than those of the other national papers with the private lives and activities of individuals, in particular of certain groups, like pop stars and sporting figures, who tend to be particularly sensitive about their public image and to have experience of legal processes. All Sunday newspapers appear to have a considerably more active libel workload than their daily counterparts. This is true in absolute, not just proportionate, terms, so the difference is particularly striking given that six dailies appear for every one Sunday production. With all Sunday papers, broadsheet and tabloid, there is a greater tendency to print material which attracts writs because of the nature of Sunday journalism, which devotes less space than daily journalism to the reporting of, and comment on, routine news and is more dependent for its impact and commercial success on investigative and exposure journalism of one kind or another.

---

[1] The complete list of those covered is as follows: the News International titles, which includes *The Times, Sunday Times, Sun, News of the World*, and *Today* (now defunct); the Mirror Group (*Daily Mirror, Sunday Mirror, Sunday People*, and *Sporting Life*); the Express Group (*Daily* and *Sunday Express*, and *Star*); *The Independent* and *Sunday Independent*, now managed as part of the Mirror Group but at the time of our study entirely separate; the *Financial Times*; and *The Guardian*.

Even though national newspapers seem to feature regularly in libel actions, particularly *causes célèbres* and those which raise new points of law, the number of actual writs served is quite small. The number of cases which come to full trial, though inevitably when they do they attract much publicity, is even smaller.[2] For example, though the *Financial Times* typically has 'two or three cases rumbling along', no one presently associated with the paper can remember it ever having been in court. A more typical daily broadsheet could have perhaps ten to twenty outstanding writs at any given time and an equivalent number of live files covering complaints related to alleged defamation initiated either by the complainant(s) themselves or by a solicitor's letter on their behalf. Even this level of formal legal proceedings would not, for a typical broadsheet daily, normally produce more than two or three cases coming to full trial in a five-year period. An active Sunday paper, broadsheet or tabloid, might have two or even three times this level of legal activity related to libel, but even so would usually only see a case come to full trial once a year or so.

Writs actually received and cases coming to trial are, however, only the tip of the libel iceberg for national newspapers. With all of them considerable and, it seems, growing, amounts of money and staff resources are devoted to the general area of libel, both before and after publication. In order to gauge the volume of this work related to libel or alleged libel after publication, it is necessary to look at the total number of files opened on complaints for whatever reason. Even here a simple count of the number of writs or letters of complaint received or cases coming to trial in any given period is not a sufficient measure of the libel workload carried by a newspaper. This is because the process of litigation is lengthy. Litigants have been able routinely to initiate proceedings up to three years after the publication of the allegedly defamatory matter and the various stages of entering pleadings and defences often themselves stretch out over years rather than months.

---

[2] Compare the analysis of judicial statistics presented in Ch. 2.

Perhaps a more informative way of looking at the extent of post-publication libel work is to count the number of files still not closed at a given moment. We were allowed to see the full current 'libel list' of two broadsheet dailies and one broadsheet Sunday paper. The Sunday paper had current files still open as a consequence of eighty-one letters of complaint and forty-one writs. The equivalent average figures for the two daily papers were forty-five cases initiated by letter of complaint and twelve by writs. These figures, though, overstate the extent of the libel problem, since it is clear that a significant number of both letters of complaint and of actual writs do not have behind them a serious intention to follow through with litigation. With the Sunday paper, of the eighty-one files begun by letters of complaint twenty-two were listed as 'dormant' and of the forty-one where actual writs had been issued twelve were also classified 'dormant'. With the daily papers the proportion of dormant 'letter cases' was also about a quarter, while the proportion of dormant 'writ cases' at two fifths was even higher than with the Sunday paper. We have no hard evidence to explain the high incidence of dormant cases, though one explanation which was suggested is that the writs are initiated in order to discourage the recipient or other newspapers from running further stories or probing into the potential plaintiff's affairs more deeply. A further informative way of indicating the scale of the libel workload of these three newspapers is to say that at the time of our interviews the daily papers regarded themselves as having an average of four cases involving active litigation that could lead to a trial if the case was not disposed of in some other way involving an out-of-court settlement, while the Sunday paper had twenty cases marked as involving 'active litigation'. Our anecdotal impression was that these figures were not out of line with the experience of the industry as a whole.

One interesting observation to emerge from an examination of the above 'libel lists', confirmed by the interviews with the other national newspapers, was that in responding to allegations of libel newspapers seem to make little distinction between those complaints that are initiated by writ and those that are initiated by letter, whether this be a personal or a solicitor's letter. The common practice seems to be to make a preliminary evaluation of all complaints, however initiated, in order to decide whether in the paper's view they have substance; if so how much substance; and then to decide upon a tactical path for handling it. We found that the incidence of robust rejections or of admissions of error, resulting in offers to print corrections and/or apologies and payments of costs and/or damages, was pretty much the same in the list examined, whether or not the case had been triggered by a writ. The process involved in each new case seemed to be, first, to take a view on its merits. This process seemed to be based on the mental exercise of deciding what would happen if the case were to come to court and what level of damages a properly directed jury would award (or which now would be sustained by the Court of Appeal), if the paper lost. On the basis of that preliminary determination tactical decisions would then be made, taking account of all the other circumstances surrounding the case in question.

Legal Procedures

We asked questions about the different arrangements that national newspapers made for handling issues involving libel, both before and after publication. These were broadly similar in the main outlines of their approach. There were arrangements in place for the editorial staff of each newspaper to have legal advice before publication. Different newspapers had slightly different internal organizational structures whereby the editor's personal control and responsibility for what appears in print is delegated for particular sections of the newspaper, so that in practice legal advice is sought and/or offered to different people at different points in the paper's production 'hierarchy': to the editor personally, to a section editor, to a production executive, to a sub-editor, or to the writers directly. In all cases, though, the doctrine governing the relationship between lawyer and journalist was that legal advice was offered which might be accepted or rejected. In practice, however, pre-publication legal advice carries heavy editorial 'clout'. A member of the editorial staff of a newspaper who ignored such advice without reference up, eventually to the editor personally, would be taking a serious personal risk.[3] If a legal adviser had reason to suppose that advice was going to be ignored, the option would be open (and would be used) of taking the issue higher up the editorial hierarchy. As a result the process of reaching agreement between journalist or editorial executive and the lawyer on the wording of what is to be published is more of a two-way discussion, even with some elements of negotiation involved. Legal advice may be sought and delivered by way of face-to-face discussion between journalist and lawyer working with a print-out of a draft article. With modern networked computer production systems an in-house legal adviser can also unilaterally 'call up' copy for consideration and enter suggested changes 'on screen' so that the writer or the sub-editor subsequently handling the article can incorporate suggestions into the text. Where outside solicitors are involved in giving pre-publication advice or clearance the working practices have always been informal. In contrast to the bulk of more normal legal work, solicitors working for newspapers give advice and discuss detailed redrafting over the telephone, though the spread of fax machines now also means that draft texts can easily be sent to legal advisers in their offices, or even increasingly to them at home.

All of the legal advisers interviewed, both those 'in-house' and those consulted in solicitors' firms, said that their advice was uniformly (if not always graciously) accepted by the journalists involved. In many contexts, of course, the legal advice was that some greater or lesser element of libel risk would attach to the publication of a particular story or article even in a redrafted

---

[3] Several respondents stated that they knew of cases in which journalists had been demoted, sacked, or not had a fixed-term contract renewed because they had led their employer into libel difficulties. Staying on the right side of the law is a matter of importance to a journalist's career.

form. In that case it was accepted that the decision whether or not to publish lay with the editor or with an appropriate editorial executive with sufficient authority to accept responsibility for the risk involved. A number of those we spoke to made the point that the character of this relationship between legal adviser and journalist depended significantly on personal factors, including in particular the relative experience of the editor or editorial executive involved in the discussion and the past libel 'track record' of the journalist writing the article.

Given this similarity of general approach to libel in all national newspapers, it is perhaps instructive to highlight the main differences between them.

All national newspapers employ in-house lawyers, except for the *Financial Times*, *The Guardian* and *The Observer*. (At the time that we were conducting our interviews, *The Independent* and the *Independent on Sunday* also had no in-house legal advice, but they now have a specific person assigned to them as part of the Mirror Group's subsequently negotiated management contract for the two titles.) The legal staffs of newspaper groups are not conspicuously large. A typical group with four or five titles employs three or four lawyers full time. They are typically expected also to do other work in addition to defamation for the title assigned to them, for example, work arising out of contempt of court, contract, copyright, or references to the Press Complaints Commission. The overwhelming bulk of the workload of an in-house lawyer, however, involves legal considerations arising out of matter being prepared for publication or with complaints and actions arising after and out of publication. With pre-publication work we were struck by the number of times that in-house lawyers stressed contempt of court rather than libel as a major concern, particularly as, apart from a small number of high profile cases, national newspapers have not been in trouble over contempt on anything like the same number of occasions as they have over libel. When asked specifically about the proportion of their time spent on libel, those responsible for daily papers replied that it took up between 30 and 40 per cent of their time, while those working with Sunday titles on average replied 'about 60 per cent'.

These average figures reflected mostly estimates of time devoted to pre-publication work and were, of course, made up of a wide variety of different working schedules. A common remark was to the effect that 'libel seems to come in waves'. With some of the Sunday titles the duty in-house lawyer would be keeping an eye on known sensitive areas of the paper under preparation and be available for consultation on an *ad hoc* basis. Then on Friday and Saturday night, as the various sections of the paper are signed off, the duty lawyer may be working continuously with draft copy from midday until the early hours of the morning.

The lower proportion of an in-house lawyer's time devoted on a daily paper to pre-publication libel issues arises from the daily production process itself. Many more of the articles printed in a daily paper have been produced from scratch, or almost from scratch, on the day itself. There is not, therefore, the same possibility of consulting the in-house lawyer during normal working hours as the writing of the story or article develops. Though there are some elements, even in daily papers, where the gestation period of an article is long- or longer-term (for example the commissioning of a profile, or a major investigation, or the printing of an extract from a book), greater reliance is inevitably placed by a daily paper on the 'night lawyering' system.

This is the system whereby lawyers come into the newspaper offices to vet copy and to be available to give advice. A night lawyer will be on duty from the early evening until after the first edition has gone to press and changes have been organized for the later editions, for example, from 5 p.m. to 8 p.m. or from 6 p.m. to 10.30 p.m., depending on the working routines of a specific paper. Some Sunday papers employ such outside duty lawyers for the full day on Saturday to deal with material that has not been 'lawyered' earlier in the week by the in-house legal staff. Night lawyers are sometimes solicitors doing 'freelance' work. On some daily newspapers they are barristers (usually younger barristers) from one of the two main libel chambers. At least one newspaper simply sub-contracts its night-lawyer roster to the clerk of one of these chambers, who then ensures that someone turns up each night. The night lawyer's responsibility is in principle to read all copy, though in practice this will mean selection and more thorough reading of some parts of the paper than others, and to be available for consultation.

At the time that we conducted our interviews, only two newspaper companies did not employ night lawyers: the *Financial Times* and *The Independent/Independent on Sunday*. In both these cases the newspapers had instead entered into a contract with a firm of solicitors with extensive libel experience by which in effect it provided pre-publication legal advice on call by telephone or fax at any time.

The two newspapers without in-house legal capacity had varying explanations for being different from the majority. The *Guardian* had no in-house lawyer concerned when it moved to London from Manchester in 1960. Instead it then established a working relationship with the solicitors' firm of Lovell, White and King (now Lovell White Durrant) which has survived for over thirty-five years. The *Financial Times* suggested that the daily contents of the newspaper have been substantially less prone to general libel activity than is the case with other national newspapers. As a matter of policy it has regarded its editorial priority as being the supply of accurate information rather than investigation and controversy. As a result it has not, so far at least, considered that the volume of work justified an in-house legal capacity. In the case of the *Financial Times*, frequent consultation by journalists and editorial executives with its retained firm of solicitors, Oswald Hickson Collier, has been positively encouraged. In the case of *The Guardian*, the overwhelming majority of pre-publication questions concerning libel has always been dealt with by one of the duty night lawyers. Pre-publication consultation with the outside solicitors is regarded as a 'rare and special event'. Thus *The Guardian* has primarily used its legal advisers in connection with writs and other issues arising after publication.

The *Financial Times* and *The Guardian* both advanced the argument that perhaps, by employing an outside firm of solicitors where ten or more experienced partners might be available, a better quality of legal advice based on a wider range of experience might be obtainable than would be the case if the paper had to rely on a single salaried lawyer, who would inevitably be overworked. A reverse view was put with greater force by the in-house lawyers of the other national newspapers. Their legal background varied. Some were ex-barristers; some were solicitors or ex-solicitors. Their view as a group was that certainly before publication and even post-publication—at least until a case began to involve the detailed setting down of defences to a writ and pleadings—their practical experience and judgement in libel matters was as extensive as that of an outside solicitor. They also argued that they gave a more 'user friendly' service to their journalists than would be provided by outside lawyers, because they saw their task very much as one of helping journalists to find ways of getting articles into the paper despite the rules of libel, rather than that of simply pointing out why a particular article or phrase could not be allowed into print because of the libel risk involved.

Indeed there seemed to be an important different of approach, even of what may be called 'culture', between the two kinds of lawyer. The in-house people see themselves, and are generally seen by the journalists they work with, as enablers. Their approach is to do what they can to get the story out unless the libel laws make it clearly impossible. The outsiders, though there is considerable variation among them, are characteristically more cautious, more concerned with ensuring that risks are avoided, although that means emasculating, or even eliminating, the story. This is particularly true of night lawyers, who are younger and less experienced. They also are in an uncomfortable 'no-win situation': they gain no kudos for taking a risk successfully, but bear the responsibility if something they approve leads to trouble.

The in-house lawyers were even more emphatic that the cost to their newspapers of employing them was substantially less than the cost would be of buying that legal advice outside. We shall say more about legal costs below. One newspaper lawyer put the point thus: 'We cost the company £250 a day and not £250 an hour.' This observation about the relative cost of in-house and external legal advice before publication is reinforced by the fact that much of the advice is required urgently and out of normal office hours. In particular the 'night-lawyer' system was seen as highly cost-effective in that in effect junior counsel's opinion was available 'on tap' in house after normal office hours at a fraction of the price that such consultation would involve through regular channels. At the time that we were doing our research, the going rate for a night lawyer was between £90 and £150 per shift, when the normal rate for a telephone discussion with a junior barrister was more like £200 per hour. In addition, of course, where a night lawyer is a barrister, the arrangements cut out the normal restriction that a barrister may only deal with a client through a solicitor.

Procedures for Handling Complaints after Publication

Complaints arising from matter published in a newspaper tend to be classified as those involving writs, those involving solicitors' letters before action, and those based on more personal complaints by letter or by telephone. In practice, so far as a newspaper is concerned, these various forms of complaint about libel overlap and merge to form a kind of continuum. Complaints can be directed in the first instance to the journalist who wrote the article, or to a section editor, or to a news desk, or to the editor directly. The main bases for complaint are alleged inaccuracy of fact and alleged unfairness of comment. Not all complaints carry with them either explicit or implicit threat of legal action. Some can be contained or satisfied by a verbal or written apology, or by publishing a Letter to the Editor, or by way of a further article, or by printing a correction. Newspapers do not make a central inventory of the total number of complaints of all kinds coming in to all first destinations, but the general impression is that a large proportion of the total number of complaints is handled in these informal ways and is often dealt with at an appropriate level in the editorial hierarchy without involving legal advisers, or even necessarily the editor, notwithstanding that issues of defamation might be involved.

Some complaints which may start off being handled in such an informal manner may become more serious from a legal point of view if, for example, the complainant is dissatisfied with the way in which the matter is being handled. Editorial executives in general are said to develop a sixth sense as to whether a particular case is about to develop into a legal case. At that point they would normally refer it to the in-house lawyer. In the cases of the *Financial Times* and *The Guardian*, the matter would be handed to the editorial executive charged with oversight of legal issues who might or might not seek advice from the paper's outside solicitors. Some letters from individuals, either from their content or tone or because of the known character of the person writing, are treated as being tantamount to a solicitor's letter before action. In general, of course, a formal solicitor's letter asserting defamation on behalf of a client, or an actual libel writ, would cause a complaint file to be opened and then its handling would be taken over by the paper's lawyer. But, conversely, some writs or threatening solicitors' letters by their content or tone are regarded as being 'try ons' and are treated accordingly with less seriousness than would be an ordinary letter of complaint with more apparent substance.

As with libel matters before publication, the doctrine governing the handling of post-publication complaints is that the newspaper lawyer is merely giving the editor advice and that the executive decision on strategy and tactics lies with the editor or with some other delegated journalist. In practice, particularly on a daily paper, the editorial staff are so engaged in bringing out the next issue that the management of complaints judged to be serious is substantially in the hands of the in-house legal team. Whether and when they bring in outside solicitors for a particular case appears to depend largely on the state of the current in-house workload. In general the in-house lawyers as a group believe that they are as good as or better than outside solicitors in the tactical handling of solicitors' letters before action or of situations created by the service of a libel writ. But if a new case breaks when the internal workload is heavy, or if it appears to raise particularly difficult or new issues, or if it appears likely to involve an unusually heavy volume of work, the in-house team may decided to pass it to an outside firm of solicitors. With the *Financial Times* and *The Guardian* all cases involving legal work would go to their respective external legal advisers. With other newspapers such work would usually be farmed out to a small handful of firms of solicitors with which the in-house legal department had established a relationship. In some cases this relationship would be more exclusively confined to one firm: for example, *The Times* for many decades has given almost all its legal work to Theodore Goddard & Co.

In responding to letters of complaint from individuals or solicitors' letters before action it appears rare for newspapers or their solicitors to take counsel's opinion. Even where a case has attracted a writ, the work involved, including advice on tactics and drafting of documents, appears to be done by in-house lawyers or on a farmed-out basis by firms of solicitors without counsel's advice, at least, as one lawyer put it to us, 'until it has got quite a long way down the track towards a trial'. There seem to be two reasons for this. The first is that experienced partners in solicitors' firms or experienced in-house lawyers regard themselves as fully qualified to give the required advice. One in-house lawyer said that, while clearly barristers have to be involved if a case looks as if it is going to trial, particularly for the drafting of the pleadings, in general in his view only the most senior barristers were in a position to contribute more to the handling of a case than he and his colleagues were already able to because 'it's a very specialized field and we are dealing with it day in and day out'. The second reason is undoubtedly cost. The legal profession in London has the reputation of being almost the most expensive in the world. At the time that we were doing our research, we were told that a conference with a QC in chambers, which might last no more than half an hour, would cost over £2,000, plus a fee of £750 to £1,000 for the junior counsel, in addition to the fee for the attending solicitor, which might also be substantial if much work was involved in preparing the brief and other documentation for the case to go to counsel. Hence a conference of this kind could end up costing between £5,000 and £10,000. There is, therefore, a reluctance to involve barristers before it is absolutely essential to do so.

Newspapers' Approaches to Dealing with Complaints

For the reasons stated at the outset of this Chapter, individual newspapers were reluctant in the extreme to discuss with us the pattern of their responses toward particular kinds of complaint, and we readily gave undertakings that we should write nothing that compromised the tactical position of an individual title or group. However, there is sufficient similarity between the way in which all national newspapers handle complaints to enable us nevertheless to make some pertinent observations.

On receiving a formal notice of complaint (or at the point when an originally tentative complaint is deemed to have become serious) the paper's lawyer makes the necessary internal enquiries so as to form a view on its objective merits. Having formed a preliminary view on whether the complaint is justified or wholly without merit or where else in the spectrum between these two extreme points it lies, he or she then also takes a preliminary view on what the outcome would be in terms of damages should the case ever come to a full trial. These preliminary exercises provide the frame for deciding on the tactics for handling each particular case. Within the basic framework the tactics for each case are decided against the background that few complaints do in fact end up in court and that, quite apart from the question of damages, the legal costs involved in actual litigation are high for both sides and rise with increasing rapidity the closer a case gets to the door of the High Court, because of the costs directly associated with preparing the documentation of a case for trial and because of the fees that have then to be paid to barristers.

All those we interviewed, accordingly, made it clear that a whole range of factors other than pure consideration of the legal merits of the case came into play in deciding tactics. Indeed the general impression conveyed was that the processes and skills deployed in dealing with cases are more like those deployed in a game of poker than those normally associated with a court of law. In particular, as in poker, there is no necessary connection between a strong or a weak hand and a satisfactory or an unsatisfactory result. Several extra-legal factors were cited to us as causing a case to be handled in a different manner from that which would be dictated by an assessment of the purely legal merits. Of particular importance were: the reputation of the complainant as a litigant; the access of the complainant to funds, since defamation does not attract legal aid;[4] whether the case would, if it came to trial, be heard in Dublin or Belfast, rather than in the High Court in London;[5] and whether time-consuming hassle could be avoided at modest expense. The above considerations, it was universally agreed, might and did induce newspapers to settle complaints in individual cases—in terms of apology, or damages, or costs, or a combination of the three—on terms more generous than was felt to be justified by the merits of the complaint. On the other side, a newspaper clearly sometimes resisted complaints where a public apology might seem to damage its editorial or commercial credibility and in other cases where it concluded that the complainant did not have the means to pursue litigation.

---

[4] As well as giving an advantage to wealthy individuals, this gives particular leverage to plaintiffs supported by the Police Federation, which reputedly maintains a seven-figure libel budget. (Whether this is accurate matters much less than the undoubted fact that belief in such a fund materially influences the way stories about police officers are handled.) Conversely, newspapers feel freer to take a harder line with less affluent individuals with no institutional backing.

[5] Juries in the two Irish jurisdictions are believed to be antagonistic to London newspapers, and to award damages in amounts reflecting that feeling.

In cases where a newspaper accepts internally that a complaint has some validity, there is a strong predisposition to settle the matter without litigation, if possible, by using informal mechanisms for their resolution. Unilateral or agreed corrections, letters to the editor, negotiated rights of reply by way of a further article, payments of modest damages either to the complainant or to a nominated charity, and payment of legal costs incurred in sending solicitors' letters were all mentioned to us as ways offered to dispose of complaints quickly and without involving the time and cost of actual litigation. One notable difference between the national and regional press is that the latter appears to show much greater willingness to apologize to complainants.[6] It remains unclear whether this reflects the greater reluctance of editors of regional papers to risk litigation or a deeply ingrained resistance on the part of national editors to ceding any sort of control over their publications. One solicitor who has negotiated on behalf of numerous plaintiffs claimed that national newspapers will trade off the prominence of their apology for money: in his example, '£10,000 and a retraction on page 5, or £2,000 plus page 1'.[7] The non-statutory Press Complaints Commission, supported and financed by the whole of the print media in the United Kingdom, with its procedures for judging complaints on the basis of a published code of conduct, was also mentioned as a way in which disputes could be settled without the involvement of litigation, particularly where the complainant was concerned with the restoration of reputation and not the winning of damages. Our impression was that most newspapers were taking this Commission more seriously than most had taken its predecessor, the Press Council.

Two instances of other attempts at the informal resolution of disputes involving alleged defamation were mentioned to us. One was an informal system whereby the in-house lawyer acted in effect as broker between a complainant and the paper's editorial

---

[6] See pp. 86–7.
[7] The sums were illustrative, and not intended to be realistic.

staff to see, without prejudice, whether it would be possible to organize an article in the paper, following on from the one complained of, which met the requirements of the complainant while at the same time being editorially acceptable to the paper. If the attempt failed on either side the complainant would then be free to return to more conventional methods of seeking redress. Others to whom we spoke were not enthusiastic about this device, which was described as 'messy'. The second unconventional method of resolution, used in one case involving a dispute over whether a particular form of words carried a defamatory meaning, was to suggest a binding arbitration by a barrister agreed by solicitors from both sides. The ruling was achieved quickly and cheaply. Rather surprisingly, in view of the general level of legal costs, arbitration of this kind does not seem to be at all common.

Journalists' Perspectives

Most of our research throughout this book focuses on the work of lawyers in what may be described as processing the law of libel on behalf of their media clients. This seemed the appropriate point of concentration because of lawyers' involvement in every context in which that law impinges, from advice at various stages on the content of what is published, through response to complaints, all the way to (and very occasionally into) the courtroom. However, it is also important to understand how libel affects those who actually produce the stories.

Journalists, particularly those working on dailies, are often remarkably difficult to get hold of for days on end. They are extremely busy, work to tight deadlines, and find it difficult to agree in advance a definite time and venue for a meeting. Our ability to arrange discussions of their experiences of libel was therefore limited. We did, however, manage interviews of varying lengths—in some instances quite extensive—with fourteen journalists. All but four held editorial positions of middle or senior rank, but some continued to write regular articles, and all had had experience as reporters. At the time of interview, they were employed on six different newspapers, although many had worked on others throughout their careers. All bar one worked on broadsheets, the great majority on dailies. However, perhaps because of the absence of an immediate deadline, two Sunday journalists provided the longest, and in many ways the most interesting, interviews.

Perhaps the most surprising finding to emerge from these interviews was the absence of complaints about the constraints of libel. We had expected smouldering, if not active, resentment against the law's fetters, and did not find it. One respondent, who had worked for several years as part of an investigative team, went so far as to say that 'Nothing I believe to be true or important enough to communicate is being left out for legal reasons', adding that 'it [libel] just means you have to be sure that what you want to say is true'. He concluded that whilst he would have been 'a crusading libel reformer' in the years before his investigative experience, he now thinks that the demands of libel law provide 'a good discipline' which a lot of journalism lacks. It requires the writer to identify witnesses and get them to provide a usable form of evidence.

One of his colleagues, asked to describe the strongest effect libel law has had on his work, responded by saying, 'As a journalist who has never been successfully sued, I've got to say I've never felt greatly burdened by the British [sic] laws of libel'. (Like numerous other people encountered in various media sectors throughout this study, he then cited Robert Maxwell as an exception.) He went on to say that 'I can think of several stories which we have modified because of libel, but I've never really thought unjustifiably, i.e. if I put myself in the person's shoes I would expect nothing less than that.' He regarded libel as reinforcing 'basic journalistic standards': 'I've always taken the view that if it's accurate then libel is not an issue and if it's not accurate we don't want to publish it anyway.'

This respondent argued that it is relatively simple to get your point across in a way that would stay within the law. A specialist in business affairs, he gave the example of a profitable company whose cash was fast disappearing. Rather than allege that the chairman was stealing the money, he would write something like, 'There are growing fears amongst the analyst community about the position of Joe Bloggs' Widgets, whose cash balances appear to [create] an uncomfortable discrepancy for investors. One institution fund manager said blah, blah.' Only if he had 'physical evidence' of the chairman's misappropriation would he make a direct accusation—yet investors, his primary audience, would get the message. He claimed to have exposed 'quite a few' malpractices and maintained that 'there are ways of doing it in which you can often pose the question, you can raise fears and doubts, you can point to discrepancies in such a way that the story is cleverly constructed, you can make a point without jumping right into the bucket.'

This example dovetailed with the view expressed by someone working in an entirely different area, that of Features. He estimated that about twice each week (on a daily paper) he had to 'tone down' the way some material was expressed. Yet he regarded the impact of libel as minimal, less even than production problems like shortage of paper. His experience has been that 'we can usually find ways to get the meaning across to readers even if we can't say it exactly as we would like to.'

Whilst the business specialist thought that libel would have greater effect where 'personalities and individuals' were involved, our one tabloid respondent equally did not bemoan the yoke of the law. She insisted that whilst everyone was always conscious of it, 'I would never not start an investigation because I was worried about the libel aspect of it.' After discussing at some length the kind of evidence required to make a story sustainable, she concluded, 'I can't actually remember a time when we haven't used a story at all in any form, because normally either we can manage to use it in some form or another or we just don't think it's true ourselves and we dropped it.'

A good proportion of her work concerned what may be called 'people stories', often relating to sex, corruption, or various dubious activities. She did say that in some cases we've probably had to water down the information that we've had and not use it as strongly as we would have liked to have done . . . because you don't actually have the proof. . . . You haven't actually caught the person in the act of something they shouldn't have been doing and therefore you have to rely on witnesses.

In her view, photographic or other documentary evidence was a great deal safer than a person's word. Even in a relatively straightforward example, that of a woman claiming to have had sex with a famous man, an editor would want corroborating evidence that the informant knew that person, and that she had been seen entering and leaving his flat or some private place to which he could be shown to be connected.

In matters of greater public importance, this caution also applied, and illustrates the difficulties of a newspaper trying to prove corruption or discreditable conduct, such as arms dealing by an individual. Even if one person is prepared to go on record with claims of having brokered an arms deal for someone, or of bribing a public official, that merely makes it a matter of one person's allegation against another, often more eminent, person's denial. Whilst this leaves the newspaper in a better position than if it merely has an informant who refuses to be taped or to swear an affidavit, it is still a long way from being able to prove the truth of the assertions, as the defence of justification requires.[8] In such an instance, our respondent was certain that the story would not run. Although the question was not put to her explicitly, it seemed that documentary evidence or multiple corroboration by credible witnesses, and possibly both, would have been required.

The perceived need for evidence of this strength may be regarded either as a valid requirement that a newspaper possess convincing proof before making damaging statements about someone, or as a legal screen behind which powerful people know they can hide to conceal wrongdoing.[9] In reality, both views are

[8] This point is developed further below.

[9] This respondent suggested that some people who engage in shady but not illegal activities deliberately arrange meetings with only one person at a time in order to protect themselves against exposure.

accurate, and not necessarily in conflict. Each may be apposite in different instances, or even with respect to different aspects of the same instance. What is quite evident is that neither this particular editor nor any of our other journalist respondents regarded the inability to publish in circumstances of this kind as an intolerable restriction on freedom of the press.

On only one newspaper did a clear indication of the inhibiting effect of libel emerge. This was the *Financial Times*, one of whose senior editors stated flatly that, as a matter of policy, the paper did not want to get involved in libel actions. Several interviewees admitted that the consequence was that they were unnecessarily cautious, particularly in their approach to stories involving misconduct by people likely to sue. The justification they offered is that the *FT*'s 'market position depends on our readers believing that what they read is right'. Consequently editors do not want to find themselves forced to issue corrections, let alone be featured on the pages of other newspapers as the loser in a libel action. The result is that the paper operates within a culture notably different from that found on any of the others we studied. Editors are less willing to take risks, and though journalists with a reputation for investigative work have been hired, their stories are always sent to a lawyer for pre-publication scrutiny. This 200 per cent concern for accuracy of information means that stories which inevitably cannot meet such exacting standards because they concern conduct which those involve take great pains to conceal do not appear in the pages of the *FT*.

Another point that emerged during the interviews was the working relationship with lawyers. This was not one of hostility; rather, most lawyers were seen as facilitators. Our respondent with investigative experience would have liked even greater involvement with lawyers, bringing them in at a fairly early stage of an investigation. He thought this would improve the chances that the story would be published, because a good lawyer would structure the investigation to get the story 'solid'. He hoped, too, that a lawyer's early participation, which would include forming a judgement about the credibility of sources, would predispose the lawyer to ensuring publication. Indeed he drew a striking analogy with the relationship (highly idealized) between the police and the Crown Prosecution Service—the journalist's draft story being the equivalent of the charge entered by the police, the lawyer shaping the final version so as to make it stick. In order to make this possible, he wanted a bigger legal department within the organization to help in this way.

This approach is, however, something of a luxury, in that it would not be of any real value to those working on a daily paper. One editor complained that, if a story is breaking and other newspapers are thought to be working on it as well, one is faced with the choice of rewriting it by editing out anything that might be 'tricky' or killing it entirely, because holding it back for two or three days to obtain strong confirmation effectively kills it as a story anyway. This inescapable dilemma may explain the sense of superiority expressed by some Sunday journalists, who regarded the work of the dailies as either that of simply recycling material or as being inevitably sloppy. However, both journalists and lawyers (not necessarily working on the same newspaper) agreed that for most stories, rewrites along the lines suggested by lawyers would enable the desired meaning to be communicated. Even the view, once taken by some journalists as an article of faith, that 'the story is no good unless you name names', no longer commands such deep adherence, since experience has shown that the substance can still be put across.

What emerged, therefore, was a sense that the journalists on the national Press felt they could work effectively within the framework of existing law. The same editor who ranked libel as a lesser difficulty than technical production problems also stated that 'we have as a response to our draconian laws devoted a great deal of ingenuity to getting round them'. Whether this is the ideal focus for the application of thought and energies may be doubted but, the *Financial Times* apart, the unanimity with which respondents insisted that nothing of importance was lost is very striking, and to an outsider persuasive. None the less the same person offered the interesting observation that libel law had made the English press 'more polemical than factual'. He meant by this to suggest that it had shaped the ethos and style of the press in general, rather than in relation to any particular story or subject. We identify below specific ways in which the threat of libel prevents or alters publication of material on certain subjects or persons. We shall return in the concluding chapter to consideration of the wider point.

The Impact of Libel on the Content of National Newspapers

One of the principal hypotheses of our research was that the libel regime as a whole was *prima facie* likely to have a 'chilling effect' on media in general. We, therefore, at every stage asked particular questions about the way and extent to which stories were either suppressed or materially altered in order to avoid or reduce libel risk, particularly if subject matter of significant public interest was involved. We have to record that, in answer to the direct question 'Are stories of public interest regularly suppressed or mutilated in your newspaper because of libel?', the answer from editors, writing journalists, in-house lawyers, and outside solicitors alike was 'No' or 'Not significantly'. As England has by general consent one of the most onerous defamation regimes in the world so far as the media are concerned—so much so that it encourages the practice of 'forum shopping', whereby litigants bring libel actions in this country which they would in many cases not be able to get off the ground in their own—this widespread reaction struck us as needing further examination.

It is clear that, in considering libel risks before publication, newspapers in general have adopted a more pro-active attitude than was the case, say, fifteen or twenty years ago. This new attitude was described to us as one of 'positive risk management'. This is not a euphemism for risk avoidance in the sense of running away.[10] Since all national newspapers are more or less in

---

[10] We argue below that financial calculations do not directly impinge on editorial decisions.

the business of challenging the authorized version of events and in questioning reputations, every newspaper every day will carry in its columns some stories with an inherent libel risk. Legal advisers see their task as that of reducing the risk to one of acceptable proportions. Part of this process involves taking steps to avoid unintended and accidental libel, such as occurs as a result of headlines and picture captions making an implication which is not justified by the text itself, or as a result of accidental juxtapositions of material, or as a result of a picture being used to illustrate a story so as to make a defamatory link between the text and a person or persons shown in the picture. The reduction or elimination of this kind of risk is achieved by careful reading of the paper as a whole before publication, and by training writers and production staff to make them more aware of the potential risks.

For the purposes of our study the more significant part of libel risk management concerns the way in which articles are written and subedited and then amended on the basis of legal advice in order to reduce risk. Here it was clear from our discussions with both the writing journalists and the lawyers that 'lawyering' of copy does result in stories being 'killed'. Sometimes this may be a major item, such as the printing of an extract from a controversial book, for example one published under the more liberal defamation climate of the United States, where it is concluded that there is a significant risk of a libel action being started and of not being able to mount a successful defence in the High Court. Sometimes it may be an inconsequential item, such as one of a number of subjects for possible inclusion in a diary which is dropped because the deadline is approaching, and in any case there is other matter that can perfectly well fill the column. More often, risk management consists of two processes: first, cutting out of the copy assertions of fact which may well be true and known to be true, but where it may be difficult or impossible to prove by way of witness statements or documents in court; and, secondly, rewriting the allegations and assertions with a view in advance of them fitting into some future defence—justification, fair comment, qualified privilege—in the event of any litigation ensuing. It has to be said on the other hand that writers who reported that their copy was watered down, redrafted, or suppressed as a result of the above considerations also willingly conceded that the process of trying to satisfy the lawyer often revealed a fundamental flaw or weakness in the investigation and writing of the article. It is also clear that journalists, particularly those with experience, are well aware of the libel regime in which they are working and, therefore, shape their research and their writing to meet its requirements. In this respect the observation that surprisingly few stories of public interest actually get suppressed or materially redrafted in light of legal advice may reflect the internalization of the restrictive norms of English libel law. This is the most effective form of censorship conceivable, one unrecognized by the writer.

In addition, lawyers and journalists who expressed the view that the libel regime was not in general significantly restrictive so far as they were concerned would also in our interviews, without any apparent sense of contradiction, list individuals or groups or kinds of material where they or their newspaper 'had to be extra careful'. The list of such sensitivities was varied but included, for example, the business activities (though not usually the private lives) of film stars and certain sports personalities; MPs who are or have been 'Names' at Lloyd's; police officers represented by the Police Federation; and copy originated abroad by agencies, correspondents, or stringers, particularly from the United States, which had been written under assumptions about constitutional protection for freedom of speech. (With another danger area, that of government and business activity in Singapore and Malaysia, the problem was the slightly different one of vulnerability to suit in the hostile courts of those countries.) Each of the newspapers we interviewed had its list of a dozen or so British public figures for whom libel warning bells always rang. The name of the late Robert Maxwell was almost invariably cited. It is hard not to conclude, at the very least, that the cumulative effect of this regime is that a significant number of stories of public interest would appear in national newspapers if editors, journalists, and their legal advisers were not conditioned by the English libel regime as a whole. It should be said, however, that the broad area of national politics and government activity is much less affected in this way than are relatively inconsequential 'people stories' and—more importantly—misconduct by private individuals and companies. It is taken as a working precept that 'politicians don't sue'.[11] Mr Jonathan Aitken, who famously resigned from the Cabinet, as someone put it, 'to spend more time with his lawyers', is a notable exception.

One final point concerning the impact of the law on what the national press can safely publish requires emphasis. It is that there exists a massive gap between what we believe most people would regard as sufficient evidence to establish the truth of a given set of facts, and what both practical realities and legal rules will permit a newspaper to rely upon for a defence in court.

By 'practical realities', we mean the problems of obtaining documentary and witness evidence sufficient to convince a jury. The difficulties canvassed briefly above were only part of the story. Some sources which purport to have first-hand knowledge of an event will do no more than speak to a journalist, and refuse to commit themselves to a written affidavit or even to be taped. Reliance on such evidence alone is clearly, and fully, recognized to be insufficient. (After all, the *Washington Post* never relied directly on 'Deep Throat' for its Watergate coverage; his disclosures were used to guide further probing by the journalists involved.) None the less where someone from inside an organization is the source, he will be understandably reluctant to jeopardize his continued employment and future prospects; few of us are strong enough to put our livelihoods at risk for the public good. Yet whistleblowers are often the only people with knowledge of crime, corruption, or unethical practices in

---

[11] This rule is understood to apply only to their conduct in office, not to matters of personal finance (e.g., the sensitivity of MPs who are Lloyd's 'Names'), or of sexual impropriety.

companies and public bodies. And, where the whistleblower is himself part of a criminal activity, he may realistically fear for his life.

Moreover, even where witnesses initially are co-operative and agree to give evidence if necessary, newspapers have in numerous instances found that ostensible pillars of support may swiftly crumble. Pressure can be brought to bear or sources can change their minds about submitting to public exposure. Newspapers cannot prevent a person leaving the jurisdiction, nor can they invoke extradition treaties to bring him back. And a witness can get cold feet at the prospect of appearing in court and undergoing cross-examination, many months, if not years, after the original disclosure, when his sense of grievance or moral outrage has cooled. For obvious reasons, someone who has himself been involved in criminal or unethical conduct has a strong disinclination to proclaim that fact and provide elaborate details on oath in open court. He can also be sure of facing an onslaught on his character as the plaintiff's counsel seeks to discredit him personally so as to destroy the credibility of his testimony.

As well as problems with witnesses, newspapers, like all media defendants, face certain legal hazards when they seek to rely on documentary evidence. Informal reports, for example those of the Securities and Investment Board on malpractice in the City, might not be entitled to qualified privilege—or so at any rate some of our respondents were advised. Hence quoting or otherwise relying on them does not protect a newspaper; if sued, it must in effect do the SIB's work over again, and then prove its accuracy to the satisfaction of the jury.[12]

Secondly—and a variant of the whistleblower problem just discussed—newspapers may find it difficult to rely on genuine documents if they are obtained by irregular means. This is

---

[12] However, an accurate report of a formal decision or finding is covered by the Sch. to the Defamation Acts 1952 and 1996. It is extremely unlikely that the SIB, or any other public body in a similar position, would voluntarily make its investigative files available to a newspaper to assist in its defence.

primarily a problem where malpractice by private parties, particularly companies, is in issue, rather than the conduct of public bodies. Here the law of libel conjoins with some much-criticized decisions of the House of Lords concerning breach of confidence and contempt of court.[13] If documents which provide evidence of improper conduct are removed surreptitiously from a company's files, it may seek return of them, ostensibly to uncover the source of the leak. Under the current law, media defendants are likely to find it impossible to resist such an action.[14] They may then find it very difficult to use material derived from those documents to help establish the truth of the stories they have published. It is unclear, and unnecessary here to attempt to explore, how the rules on discovery might assist or hinder investigative journalism. However, we were told of one important story which would have exposed fraud concerning statements in the prospectus of a well-known company responsible for a major international facility, but which had to be seriously watered down because the newspaper received legal advice that it would not be allowed to retain the leaked confidential documents on which the allegations were based. Believing that the newspaper would therefore be unable to prove justification, the journalist rewrote the story from a different and less critical angle.

The Influence of Financial Considerations

It is important to distinguish among the various effects that the costs of libel may have. We were told by everyone to whom the question was put, and found no evidence whatever to the contrary, that, whilst editors and lawyers seek in general to avoid

---

[13] *British Steel Corpn.* v. *Granada Television Ltd* [1981] AC 1096, and *X Ltd* v. *Morgan-Grampian (Publishers) Ltd* [1991] 1 AC 1.

[14] The *Morgan-Grampian* case went to the European Court of Human Rights, which held that the court's order for return of the documents breached the journalist's freedom of expression under Art. 10 of the Convention: *Goodwin* v. *United Kingdom* (1996) 22 EHRR 123. It is unclear at the time of writing whether and how the relevant law will be amended in response.

falling foul of the law, they never attempt even rough financial calculations about what a particular story might cost. Nor do they take policy decisions based on pounds and pence—for example, to refuse to undertake investigative journalism, where the perils of libel are inevitably much greater. In this respect, their behaviour contrasts markedly with book publishers, as will be seen in Chapter 6.

Moreover, there is a competitive spirit amongst journalists which in certain quite common circumstances will prevail over the caution that a purely economic risk-based calculation would produce. For example, when one newspaper runs a story, the others seem to feel obliged to print something similar and then try to develop it further. This attitude seems a mixture of an unwillingness to be outdone by a rival (which might hurt circulation and therefore is at bottom an economic factor) and what may be called professional pride, embodied in the idea that one story is never definitive and a good journalist should be able to find more or squeeze more out of existing sources.

Moreover, it seemed to us as though sometimes the sheer excitement of having access to a story, particularly an exclusive, can lead to a sort of collective rush of blood to the head and a decision to publish a story without the degree of confidence in the truth of the underlying facts that would normally be demanded. 'People stories' are the most likely to be treated in this way. A prime example is the 'World exclusive' claimed by the *Daily Mirror* which purported to detail Elton John's 'diet of death'. This story, which originated in copy submitted solely to the Mirror by a free-lance contributor in Los Angeles, was purportedly based on observations by two gatecrashers at a Hollywood party. In reality it seems largely to have been fabricated by the free-lance himself. The newspaper's failure to verify was so gross that the Court of Appeal had no difficulty in upholding a finding of recklessness so as to support an award of exemplary damages.[15]

This sort of conduct, and the attitude it reflects, seem to us to

[15] *John* v. *MGN Ltd* [1996] 2 All ER 35.

be distinctive to the national press, or at any rate to sections of it, and to have no parallel in other media. Local newspapers (see Chapter 4) would be frightened off by the potentially crippling cost of losing a lawsuit brought on by lack of care in verification. Television broadcasters, conditioned by the regulatory culture which has shaped the industry since its inception (see Chapter 5), would also find such a buccaneering approach alien to their way of operating. Chancing one's arm to beat the competition seems to be the sole prerogative of high-profile, high-turnover, high-volume enterprises which are not responsible to any public authority—and, perhaps fortunately for all those affected (including the national newspapers themselves), rare enough even for them.

However, though financial calculation may carry little weight in influencing national newspapers' output, the matter is very different when it comes to handling, and especially to settling, complaints of libel. It is worth recalling Professor Patrick Atiyah's observation, first made many years ago, that 'a settlement is a business bargain in which the plaintiff sells his claim to a private buyer for what he can get, and the buyer buys for as little as he has to pay'.[16] It is a golden rule of civil litigation that most cases settle and virtually no one wants to end up in court. Libel, however, exhibits this tendency to the most extreme degree. Most complainants seek only modest compensation and, as with all negotiations, usually come away with less than they request. The headline-making cases of 'telephone-number' jury awards are very rare indeed: that is why they make headlines. Very few awards reach six figures, and although no one was willing to supply statistics, all the lawyers willing to discuss the matter in general terms emphasized that most claims are settled for under five figures. Indeed many people are happy with no money so long as they receive a correction or apology. A national newspaper

---

[16] P. Atiyah, *Accidents, Compensation and the Law* (4th edn. by P. Cane, Butterworths, London, 1987), 274. This remark, which appears in all earlier editions going back to 1970, seems to have vanished from the latest (1993) edition.

may resist a complaint because, rightly or wrongly, it regards the claim as being without merit, but unlike its regional counterparts, in most cases it will not be unduly worried about the amount of damages in issue.

What *will* give it great pause, however, are the legal costs involved in resisting a claim. The absence of reliable and extensive empirical data precludes authoritative statements, and the whole subject of negotiated settlements in civil cases badly needs more extensive study than it has yet to receive.[17] None the less we came away with the strong impression that the level of legal costs in libel cases is more out of proportion to the money received by complainants—which is ultimately what the parties are litigating about—than in any other area of law. There is thus a particularly strong incentive to try to curtail litigation in its earliest possible stage, before costs become serious. Above all, this means trying to avoid the need for barristers, whose involvement escalates costs dramatically[18] and whose services must be employed from the pleading stage onwards.

The high ratio of costs to awards seems to result from the unparalleled technicality of libel law, which encourages a greater number of pre-trial pleading issues and discovery motions than are found in other areas of law. Costs therefore mount up earlier in libel litigation than in other civil disputes. To continue the poker analogy used earlier in this Chapter, this may have the effect of inducing newspaper defendants to 'fold' a hand that might well be strong enough to win, but only at the risk of a very large loss if it fails. If they 'fold' early in the game, the loss is relatively small and can be easily absorbed. The result is that, so

---

[17] The leading British study is H. Genn, *Hard Bargaining* (Clarendon Press, Oxford, 1987), which looked at out-of-court personal injury settlements. See also J. Phillips and K. Hawkins, 'Some Economic Aspects of the Settlement Process: A Study of Personal Injury Claims' (1976) 39 *MLR* 497. There is a much larger American literature, but it is of limited relevance because of the radically different structure of litigation in all jurisdictions there, notably the fact that each party bears its own cost, regardless of result, and also the operation of the contingency fee system.

[18] See the figures quoted at p. 54 above.

long as they avoid attracting a reputation of being 'a soft touch', newspapers will frequently agree to settle cases they regard as unmeritorious for a small sum, provided they do not regard any important principle as being at stake.

One way to minimize economic risk, of course, is to take out insurance. In the present context, however, the danger is that insurers will insist upon behaviour that minimizes risk. Harry Evans when editor of *The Sunday Times* in the 1970s, famously refused to carry insurance for fear that pressure might be brought on his editorial decisions. Yet respondents were unequivocal: insurers exercise no influence on decisions about publication. Beyond that, information was difficult to prise out of them— some did not want it revealed publicly whether their papers or clients even carried insurance. From what we could glean, however, it appears that insurers in some limited instances may influence the process of settlement. This influence is more often only indirect: one in-house lawyer said that, whilst he did not feel under constant pressure from them to treat any case in any particular way, he was always aware that the insurers were 'in the background'. However, a more direct form of influence may be exerted when the insurer's representative advises a settlement: the paper is free to reject this advice, but the insurer then no longer covers the risk, so if a case is lost in court or settled more expensively later on, the cost falls on the newspaper itself. One important reason for the minimal influence of insurers is that all policies prescribe a very substantial excess—the amount below which the newspaper, like any insured party, must bear the costs itself. That sum is generally so high that most awards and virtually all settlements are not covered, even though legal costs are also included.

Conclusions

The law of libel as it impinges upon newspapers, and indeed upon all media, may be seen from three different angles: as a normal *business cost*; as an *obstacle to be got round*; or as an *effective deterrent* to the publication of certain material. Our research suggests that the first two aspects are the most important with respect to the national Press, and we have tried to describe how they influence newspapers' daily operations. We have also shown that, though the third form of impact is of lesser importance in this sphere, it does exist and exerts influence in ways that working journalists may not themselves fully appreciate.

Although there are relatively few full trials involving national newspapers, libel work of one kind or another bulks large. It is worth re-emphasizing a point made early in this Chapter: that libel trials, or even writs, are really a minor part of the impact of the law. Most of the resources newspapers devote to libel are expended on pre-publication 'risk management', and secondly on post-publication response to complaints. The latter is an elaborate negotiation exercise which attempts to prevent complaints developing into writs and, where that proves unsuccessful, to the great poker game of arriving at out-of-court settlements, preferably early enough to avoid massive legal costs.

Another factor accounting for the importance of defamation to the national press is that, partly for commercial and editorial reasons related to the highly competitive and crowded nature of the industry, they feel themselves under pressure to push at the boundaries of what is possible in terms both of writing about the private lives of public figures, and of investigating public life. Moreover, editors and, it has to be said, some of the legal advisers of national newspapers are not concerned solely with profit maximization. They see it as part of their function and derive some of their professional satisfaction from being involved in making case law. Such cases run for years and cost seven-figure sums by the end. One will suffice to make the point. The litigation between Derbyshire County Council and its then leader, David Bookbinder, against the *Sunday Times* began with an article and a libel writ in the autumn of 1989, arising out of allegations of misuse of pension-fund money. One major but preliminary issue of law—whether a local council can sue for defamation—was not finally determined until 1993, in the House of Lords. The final settlement, involving damages and costs to Mr Bookbinder, was not agreed until the spring of 1996. Even without such high peaks of litigation, national newspapers are involved in regular libel activity where the annual budget provision for, say, a daily paper and its Sunday sister will be over £1 million. We found no evidence that this sum as a budgetary item loomed over the editor or the journalists on national newspapers in such a way as to inhibit or deflect their editorial judgements or decisions. It is, however, a rough measure of the importance of libel in general in the life of national newspapers.

We recorded one striking observation by an in-house lawyer of wide experience. He said, 'When big cases go wrong, there is a sudden flurry of memos and editors saying we must tighten up. But that really is pointless, because it's like asking a Grand Prix racing driver to stop crashing cars.' In other words, if they are doing their job properly, libel is inescapably part of the business which the national media are engaged in.

An unsympathetic critic of the national press might argue that it would not have such a libel problem if it showed greater regard for factual accuracy and confined what it wrote to what it could prove to be true. This line of criticism misses the essential nature of journalism, which involves the daily or weekly publication by a title of the same number of words as are to be found in an average full-length novel, produced against tight and inflexible deadlines. Further, in order to have a defence against every possible defamation it is not enough for the newspaper to have reached a responsible judgement that an assertion is true. It would require certainty that in every case there were witnesses willing and able to appear in court on the paper's behalf, or that conclusive and legally admissible documentary evidence be in the editor's hands. If such certainty were required for everything controversial, there would be no newspapers worth reading.

4

Regional Newspapers

Introduction

In contrast to national newspapers the principal research method
for the regional press was a questionnaire, devised by us, but sent
out on our behalf by the Newspaper Society and the Guild of
Editors. We further interviewed some editors and assistant
editors of particular newspapers in person or over the telephone.
Our object was to ascertain the impact of defamation law on
regional and local papers. In particular, we were interested to find
out how this differed from that experienced by national newspapers. Comparisons may also be drawn with the experience of
magazines which have a national circulation, but which like many
regional papers are issued weekly (or monthly). Our initial
hypothesis was that the incidence of libel writs and complaints is
much lower than it is in the case of the London papers, although
we did not assume that, as a result, this area of law has less overall
impact on the regional press.

The questionnaire was sent out in March 1994, with replies
requested for 31 May 1994. It was sent out to 250 regional editors,
members of the Guild of Editors. There were forty-four responses
from editors, assistant editors, or in some cases group editors,
representing 118 newspaper titles. Six titles were morning papers,
twenty-two evening papers, twenty-seven paid for weekly papers,
and four were Sunday newspapers. Of the other titles, fifty-eight
were weekly free papers and one was a monthly business
publication. The questionnaire was designed in the first place to
elicit some information about the number of writs in the previous
five years (1988–93), about the number of cases which came to

court in that period, and about the approximate number of complaints received annually. We were also interested in how complaints were dealt with, the impact of defamation law on various types of story or feature, and the reasons which impel editors not to publish or significantly to amend a story. We were also interested in some insurance and financial aspects: what, if any, insurance arrangements were made, the level of premiums, and the influence of insurers on the conduct of actions. Finally, we were interested in the editors' impressions concerning the overall impact of libel law on their newspapers and how this might differ from that experienced by the national press.

As already mentioned, we interviewed a number of editors, in some cases asking them to supplement the answers given in response to the questionnaire. Some other interviews were conducted to obtain more complete information.

Statistical Information

Respondents were invited to answer a number of straightforward questions concerning the number of defamation actions and cases in the previous five years, 1988–93, and their outcome. There was a very full answer to the first question concerning the number of writs during this period, but many respondents did not answer other questions about the number of cases which came to court, the number which were settled, etc. It is very likely that editors (or their assistants) regarded these further questions as in a sense inapplicable in view of the absence of any libel litigation during the period under consideration.

Table 1. *Number of writs issued against newspaper(s) in the five years 1988–93*

None (or no answer)	17
1–5	24
6–10	1
11–20	1
21	1

In other words, an overwhelming majority of respondents had received five or fewer writs during a five year period, and over one third of them (seventeen out of forty-four) had received none at all (or in two instances gave no answer to this question).

The next group of questions were concerned with litigation during the same period: how many cases came to court and with what result, and what happened to other cases? Of course, these cases would not necessarily result from writs issued in the same period. They might have been taken out some years previously, while proceedings for which a writ was issued in, say, 1988 or 1989 might have remained inactive during the period under review. Only four respondents reported that libel actions had come to trial during that period. In two cases damages were awarded against the newspaper, in one case £9,000 and in the other £3,700. In the third there was a settlement during the course of proceedings, and the fourth was continuing at the time of response.

Twenty-four respondents reported that actions had been settled before they came to court; one group of newspapers had settled twenty-five actions and another fifteen. The terms of settlement varied considerably: two payments of £40,000 or more were made, and one group reported a settlement of £15,000 and two other payments of £10,000 each. But payments ranging from £750 to £5,000 were much more common. In most cases it was stated that costs were also paid. In a few an apology was published or a statement made in open court. In one case a free full page advertisement was printed as a means of rectification of the libel.

Eight respondents replied that the action had been discontinued by the plaintiff. In two instances this occurred because he had become bankrupt. But in many more cases (thirty-seven to thirty-nine) the writ was withdrawn after the newspaper apologized, and in about 50 per cent of these cases it also paid the plaintiff's costs. In a handful of instances actions were discontinued for other reasons, e.g, because the plaintiff died or apparently lost all interest in the case.

We also asked about the approximate number of letters before action or other threats of libel proceedings which were received or made *annually*. (We did not think it would be reasonable to expect precise information on this matter, and it seemed better to ask for an annual estimate, rather than ask about the five previous years.) Information was also requested about the source of these complaints.

Table 2. *Approximate annual number of letters and telephone calls with a serious threat of legal action*

	The number of reported communications				
	None	1–5	6–10	11–20	20+
Solicitors' letters	3	15	11	10	1
Individuals' letters	5	14	12	5	4
Organizations' letters	14	21	–	5	–
Telephone calls	9	15	7	5	4

These figures do not bring out some important contrasts. For instance, an executive editor responsible for two leading city newspapers, one morning and one evening, reported that there were about thirty complaints annually from solicitors, fifty from individuals, and about 100 telephone calls which made a serious threat of libel proceedings. At the other end of the scale, a local free weekly paper said it had received only two letters from solicitors over the last nine years and no other complaints at all! Another point is that some papers reported a significantly higher incidence of complaints from solicitors than individuals; one evening paper with a high degree generally of libel activity said that 80 per cent of complaints came from solicitors, while only 5 per cent came from individuals. In contrast, another said there were 'dozens' from the latter and only two or three letters a year from solicitors.

The most interesting point is the marked difference between the number of complaints, however made, and the number of writs. Editors were asked what proportion of complaints are resolved informally. The answers are reproduced in Table 3 below.

Table 3. *Proportion of complaints resolved informally*

Less than 60%	1
61–70%	3
71–80%	1
71–80%	2
More than 90%	33

The overwhelming majority of the respondents (forty out of forty-four) to this question, therefore, reported that over 90 per cent of complaints were resolved informally (by methods described a little later in this chapter). Indeed, many members of this group said that all complaints were resolved informally, while others referred to 'nearly all' or '95 per cent +' as being resolved in this way. There was only one seriously divergent answer which came from a morning paper, where there had been a large number of writs (ten) in the five year period: it reported that only 50 per cent of complaints were resolved informally.

Legal Advice and Procedures for Dealing with Claims

In the second part of the questionnaire a number of questions were asked about the use of lawyers and other sources of legal advice, both prior to publication and in dealing with complaints. We were also interested to find about the procedures which were used to resolve complaints informally, and in particular about the person who took responsibility for investigating the story's accuracy at the complaints stage. Finally, we asked what factors were influential in determining whether to offer an apology, settle or fight a case.

1. Legal and other advice

Editors were asked whether their newspaper employed in-house lawyers, a standard (though not universal) practice in the case of national papers and broadcasting companies. All except three said they did not employ in-house lawyers. Moreover, none of them contemplated taking this step. In addition to the three with in-house advice, two editors whose papers belonged to a large press group said they turned to the group lawyer for advice. However, the majority of those without access to in-house or group legal advice (twenty-seven out of thirty-nine) consulted a firm of solicitors before deciding whether to publish a story. Seventeen respondents said they did this regularly, while others said such consultation is infrequent—only three or four times a year or 'twelve times at most'. One experienced editor said that it was advisable for insurance reasons to consult a solicitor before publishing a story with obvious libel risks. But pre-publication consultation is not legally required under the insurance contract.

On the other hand, some editors said they were reluctant to contact lawyers. They pointed out that they and their journalists were experienced about libel dangers, and knew when it was too risky to publish. One editor wrote: 'All of our journalists are taught the law of defamation, and we are paid to make our own judgements.'

Respondents were also asked whether they sought the advice of the Newspaper Society or other body before publication. Fifteen replied that they did, and seven said they did not. But it was emphasized in three detailed replies that the Newspaper Society's advice was sought on points of principle or procedural matters, rather than on whether it was wise to publish a particular story. Only one other (local) advice centre was specifically mentioned.

2. *Procedures in dealing with claims*

We first asked a number of related questions under this heading:
—What is the procedure when there is a threat of legal proceedings?
—Do you always immediately call on a solicitor, the Newspaper Society, or other body for assistance?
—Is that required by your insurance policy?

The questions elicited a variety of responses. Eight respondents emphasized that it was not automatic to refer the threat to solicitors immediately; there was initially an in-house investigation, and a reference would only be made when it was clear that there were difficulties in dealing with it. But two of these respondents added that if the complaint came from a solicitor, it would be always be referred to the newspaper's solicitor.

Twenty-six (of the forty-four) respondents said that a solicitor would be called in, at any rate when it was clear that the complaint was a serious one. Fifteen of them added that this was a requirement under their insurance policies. Four respondents used staff at the Newspaper Society in these circumstances. One interviewee, however, preferred to avoid solicitors whenever possible. Unless there was a writ or the complainant was unusually persistent, he almost invariably decided how to handle the complaint: '99 per cent of the time I steer away from lawyers because they are so expensive.'

Whether a complaint is referred to a solicitor or not, it must be investigated to determined whether it is well-founded or whether the allegedly defamatory story is accurate (or fair comment, etc.). This is clearly an essential step before it can be decided whether to offer an apology or correction, or alternatively contest the allegation. We asked which person or persons had this responsibility. The answers are tabulated in Table 4.

Table 4. *Responsibility for investigating accuracy of stories*

Editor	18
Deputy Editor	13
Editor and lawyers	4
Departmental Head/News Editor	3
Paper (unspecified personnel)	4

Some editors, it seems, spend a considerable amount of time investigating and dealing with libel complaints and other related matters. One experienced editor estimated this amounted on average to be about half an hour to an hour a day, though another doubted whether it came to more than an hour or so a week. Many emphasized that it was their responsibility to deal with the complainant, even if the initial in-house investigation was conducted by a senior member of the staff.

We also asked how often counsel had been called on in the last five years to advise whether to settle or contest. Twenty-six respondents said that they asked for counsel's opinion, while fourteen said that they had not asked for an opinion from the Bar. In most cases, twenty-one, an opinion had been obtained on only one to five occasions, but one paper said a barrister had been consulted on thirty separate cases and another referred to some fifteen to twenty consultations.

More broadly we asked what factors determined whether the newspaper would offer an apology or some other settlement, or decide to contest the claim. Were they primarily legal, financial, or a combination of factors? Not surprisingly thirty respondents gave the last answer. Seven said that legal considerations were primary, while only two considered financial factors paramount. The answers to this question were for the most part anodyne, and perhaps this was inevitable, given its vague character. It may be surmised that the weight of factors varies considerably from case to case. Some answers, however, were more specific and helpful. The editor of one important Sunday paper said that 'sometimes an apology is carried, even though we are confident a writ could be successfully defended, to head off possible legal costs'. A similar point was made by the editor of a morning paper who wrote that sometimes 'it is cheaper to pay a relatively low compensation claim out of court than to proceed and risk much higher damages should the case fail'. A third answer was to the effect that the cost of fighting had to be weighed against the cost of settlement; normally the insurer's recommendation would be accepted. (The influence of insurance companies is discussed later.) A fourth response emphasized that the paper would only get into a fight with commercial risk if there was a 'vital point of principle' at stake. Two replies said that the means of the plaintiff would be taken into account.

3. The informal resolution of complaints

As stated earlier the overwhelming majority of complaints are resolved informally by editors. The questionnaire invited editors to explain how this was done; this elicited some very full answers. For the most part, respondents stated firmly that if they got the facts wrong, they were willing to publish an apology or correction. Typically the editor replied, sometimes (it was said) over the telephone, after a preliminary investigation of the facts. If it was appropriate to publish a correction or apology, its terms were negotiated with the complainant. In other cases the newspaper might offer to publish a letter in reply or a balancing article. Where the complaint was unwarranted, an informal discussion over the telephone might persuade the complainant to drop the matter. He might, according to one editor, be referred to the Press Complaint Commission. In interview an editor said that he would provide a right of reply if the complainant had an apparently reasonable case, or a request for one came from a solicitor—though the paper would probably consult its own lawyer. The flavour of these answers is best given by some quotations from replies to the questionnaire:

We state in every issue our willingness to publish clarifications, corrections and, where appropriate, apologies. We act on this—negotiating whether they appear as a letter or in the body of the news pages, and with what prominence. As long as these don't appear too often, more than once a month say, then I believe this *adds* to our image of fairness and even-handedness rather than damaging credibility (Editor's own emphasis).

We reply to each complaint individually after first making preliminary enquiries of the member(s) of staff concerned. If corrections or explanations are appropriate, we agree them with the complainant, taking legal advice if necessary, before publication.

[All complaints are resolved informally] with telephone call to talk matter through and decide amicably whether correction or apology should be published or whether it was just a need to let off steam. A letter would follow up agreement for wording of apology to serious complaint or solicitor's letter. Advice given where appropriate about the PCC.

Most people want either an apology or correction—which we carry, provided the fault lies with our reporting or headline writing. People also want to hear someone say sorry.

The Impact on the Content of Regional Papers

We explored the extent of the impact of libel law in both the questionnaire and in our interviews. We were, for example, interested to discover what types of item carried significant libel risks and the reasons for a decision to drop or amend them. We hoped that editors could give us some idea of the particular stories they had not reported as fully as they would have liked.

The first question in this section of the questionnaire invited editors to tell us how many stories of public interest in their community had not been covered at all in the five years, 1988–93, or had been significantly amended. As the questionnaire itself admitted, this is inevitably a matter of subjective impression and we did not expect a precise answer. Indeed, a few responses (out of forty-four) simply said in answer to the question about total non-coverage: 'one or two', 'a few', or 'several'. Equally, they tended to say in answer to the question about the number of items significantly amended: 'many', 'lots', or in one case 'innumerable'. But the majority of responses did give a relatively precise answer, summarized in Table 5.

Table 5. *The approximate number of stories of public interest not covered and significantly amended over 5 year period 1988–93*

	None	1–5	6–10	11–20	21+
Not covered	20	11	2	3	–
Amended	14	9	4	2	2*

* One editor said about 50 stories had been amended in this way

Without doubt the most interesting, and also surprising, aspect of these figures is that almost half the respondents (twenty out of forty-four) denied they had ever suppressed or not covered a story because of the impact of defamation law. Indeed, almost a third said they had not had significantly to change a story for that reason. Many of these replies came from editors who also reported that they annually received a number of complaints, or had received some writs during the past five years, in respect of defamation. The answers may suggest that these editors are not deterred, or chilled, much by libel laws and are always prepared to publish a story of real public interest, despite the risk of a complaint. The other explanation is that whatever their practice many editors are reluctant to admit that they do not cover or suppress stories, or even that they amend them in a radical way. This second conclusion would be more compatible with what we found with other branches of the media. It also fits with the impression gained in some interviews that, after some initial hesitation, editors do admit that they frequently kill the investigation of a story at an early stage because of its libel risks. As one editor said:

you are not going to let a reporter spend three months on a story that you are convinced is going to be spiked because it is leaky and dodgy. Because of financial restraints on your resources you just don't embark on that procedure in the first place. So to say that stories have been spiked is the wrong nuance really.

In other words, it is not only or primarily a matter of suppressing a report which has been drafted, but a matter also of not investigating a story which clearly has libel implications.

Equally some editors (either in writing or interview) supplemented their answers by pointing out that they were always concerned to publish an important story in some form, and their main concern was to do this in a way which was, so far as possible, libel-proof. One said that his concern was not whether to publish, but about 'how to publish stories safely'. It was only when the journalist had not been able to persuade him that the story could be 'stood up' that he would stop its publication. Another replied that very few stories were not reported at all, but significant or slight amendments were made every day to the text of the paper.

Secondly, we asked editors to answer a number of questions on the assumption (which was warranted) that a number of them in some instances stopped or amended stories on the basis of a libel risk. We invited them in the first instance to provide a brief description of some major stories which had never been reported or had been significantly amended for that reason. Most of them replied in general terms, referring, for example, to stories concerning head-teachers of schools, police and prison officers, or local government officials. The financial problems of local businesses, including football clubs and farms, also received one or two mentions. Only a small minority of replies was more detailed. One reported that stories about a religious group and about the management of a council-owned concert hall had both been dropped because of difficulties in obtaining enough evidence to justify them in the event of a libel action. Another referred to a scandal concerning time share holiday letting, while a third mentioned that a story about the sudden resignation of a headmaster of a girls' school on supposed 'health grounds' had never been fully reported.

25% of the responses (eleven out of forty-four) highlighted stories concerning the police as among those which were most frequently suppressed or altered. One editor said that they had become restricted 'to information based on statements by senior officers of police' which might attract qualified privilege under provisions of the Defamation Act 1952 (then in force). Another reported to similar effect:

Allegations of violence and bad behaviour by officers, unsupported by very reliable and preferably numerous witnesses are avoided. As well as firm evidence of bad behaviour, we would also hope to have an official police quote confirming it, or an inquiry, before publishing.

On the other hand, in interview two other editors bracketed stories about members of other groups, for example, head teachers and town hall workers, with allegations about the police: the common factor is that they were all represented by 'associations which are known to be very prepared to go to court on behalf of their members or clients'. We did not find the expression of this view surprising. The willingness of bodies such as the Police Federation to support members' libel actions is well-known, and we received the same reaction from other sectors of the media. On the other hand, it was striking, and on one perspective disquieting, to hear how far this inhibited the regional press. One editor who was interviewed said that he frequently dropped sports stories, because their content (in his view) was often not sufficiently important to run the risk of an action: 'the story is not that important to risk even a few thousand pounds worth of libel costs'.

We also asked editors what sorts of items in their newspaper were likely to carry significant libel risks. The answers set out in Table 6 corroborate the responses to other questions.

Table 6. *What items in your newspaper are likely to carry significant libel risks? Editors could mention more than one item*

Political reports (local/national)	16
Reports of local crime, police investigations courts cases	29
Sports pages	10
Local theatre, arts, etc.	4
Business and financial items	21
Letters page	26
Adverts and notices	8

A few replies added other items not mentioned in the question: gossip columns, 'anything that affects members of the Police Federation and senior Council officials', investigations. Seventeen (of the forty-four) replies mentioned three or more items, and three ticked all seven items! What was most interesting was the prominence given to the libel risks posed by letters pages. In interview editors pointed out the difficulties in checking whether the correspondent had got the facts right and expressed their reluctance to publish a letter unless they were confident that this was the case.

We also asked editors to indicate the major reasons for deciding not to publish or to amend a story, though we suggested that inevitably there would be some overlap between these heads.

Table 7. *What are the major reasons for deciding not to publish or to amend a story?*

Absence of evidence	37
Doubts about proving truth	31
Case too expensive to fight	10
General financial and management constraints	8

Five replies mentioned other reasons, such as the shortage of staff to do a proper investigation of the story, or a suspicion that their journalist has been fed an inaccurate or malicious story. One editor said that sometimes a story would be withheld if its publication would occasion embarrassment or damage a business. What clearly emerges from these answers is that editors feel that legal and evidential considerations play a much greater part than financial or management factors in deciding what to publish. However, a somewhat different impression was given by the editors who were interviewed. They emphasized that in every case they considered the importance of the story, whether its truth could be proved (if a case came to court), and the costs to the newspaper. One editor admitted he was 'extremely cost-conscious because the sums of money in terms of everything else that we do in our normal day to day lives is so extraordinarily high'. For another, 'there is a constant weighing up of resources against the possible benefits of a story'.

How are Local Papers More or Less Vulnerable than Nationals?

We asked the editors in what ways they considered that a local newspaper might be more or less vulnerable than a national paper to libel risks. This was a deliberately open-ended question. We did not assume that local papers were or were not more vulnerable than nationals. We left space on the questionnaire form for a full answer.

There was a variety of interesting replies. A clear majority (twenty-four out of forty-four) considered local papers more vulnerable. The principal reason suggested for the difference was the perception on the part of the public that local papers do not have the resources to fight a libel action and are, therefore, prepared to settle as quickly and cheaply as possible. Moreover, for some people a defamatory slur in a widely-read local paper would be more injurious than an item in a national which might not have a large circulation in the particular community. One editor referred to an instance where a local paper had been sued in respect of a story which had also been published at the same time by the *Daily Mirror* and the *Daily Express*; no proceedings had been taken against either national paper. A third point was that local papers usually do not have in-house lawyers to vet copy before publication. Finally, a few members of this first group of editors argued that, after some high profile celebrity awards or settlements against the nationals, complainants thought they could try their hand and get similar sums of money from local papers. Here are a few representative comments:

Complainants tend to think there is more chance taking action against regional/local papers because they perceive us having less resources and therefore 'weaker' than the nationals. We are also more accessible because of our concentrated readership and lifestyle in the areas that matter.

I suspect that regional papers are more vulnerable, because, on the whole, they have less money behind them. This makes regional papers generally more cautious about stories involving a risk of libel.

Regional papers cannot afford to run 'good stories' taking libel costs in their stride. The costs even in cases settled out of court can be prohibitive, e.g., £10,000—a relatively low sum—amounts to two-thirds of a reporter's annual salary.

The fear is always present that a big libel loss will prove terminal.

However, another view was put by a minority of respondents (six out of forty-four). This was that a local paper is very sensitive to its own standing in the community and therefore avoids the publication of defamatory material; this might have an adverse impact on its circulation. Two editors thought their type of weekly newspaper was also less inclined to engage in investigative journalism than daily or Sunday nationals and so carried fewer stories with libel risks. An executive editor said that his papers were not under the same competitive pressures as (some of) the nationals to engage in risky sensational journalism. Three editors considered their papers less vulnerable, because they took great care to research their stories or because they knew the people concerned. The minority view is well represented by these quotations:

Less vulnerable in the fact that we are not so actively looking for scandal stories and are also closer to sources of information.

Generally, 'community' based papers such as ours do not undertake investigative journalism. Thus the risks are lessened.

But a third group of replies concluded local papers are both more and less vulnerable than the nationals. They are more vulnerable in the sense that the financial repercussions of a libel action or settlement may be drastic, particularly for a small paper. But these prospects induce their editors and journalists to take greater care or to avoid sensitive topics, which makes them in another sense less vulnerable. This perspective was shared by about five or six replies, from which two quotations are taken:

So far as we can judge, we are neither more nor less vulnerable than national newspapers, although we suspect more local people would be willing to challenge us than they would a 'giant'. Also, we are unlikely to risk libel knowingly, whereas a national might consider potential damages worth a gamble in the right circumstances.

The absence of on-hand, immediate and automatic legal advice make local and regional papers *more* susceptible but the absence of malice, perceived lack of resources and better links with the community make it more likely that local papers will get away with it.

The second of these answers was to some extent qualified in interview: local papers enjoy an amicable relationship with their community, and until recently have rarely been required to pay damages. On the other hand, editors were very sensitive about the standing of their paper and would at all costs avoid getting a name for publishing defamatory matter which could not be justified.

Although these answers may appear to conflict, we think some conclusions can safely be drawn. First, editors are heavily influenced by the possible financial repercussions of a libel action and so take very few risks, compared to their peers in national papers. As one editor who had previously worked on a national paper put it, 'you don't take any chances within the context of a regional paper, whereas the job I did at [a popular Sunday national] was basically all high risk'. It follows, secondly, that regional papers in contrast to nationals are most unlikely to publish a defamatory story, knowingly accepting the risk that they will be sued and have to pay up. Finally, we conclude they do seem to be less exposed to the risk of being sued and in that sense are less vulnerable than national papers. But this is largely attributable to their greater financial vulnerability, which inhibits them from taking risks which in some circumstances national papers may be prepared to incur.

Insurance Arrangements

We asked editors a number of questions about their insurance arrangements. Regrettably, the answers were rarely very helpful, and it may be conjectured that editors are often uninterested in, or ignorant of, the terms of their insurance policies and their premiums. We also interviewed some libel insurers and a solicitor who acted for one of them, as well as examining some typical policies. Five editors said they took out individual insurance policies, while eighteen were covered by group policies. Thirteen were insured by the Newspapers Mutual Insurance Society (NMIS), while seven respondents, members of the Pearson Group (which includes the Westminster Press), were insured with

Cigna Insurance. Three other group insurance arrangements were mentioned. Four editors, two of them editing associated papers in the same group, replied that it was company policy not to take out libel insurance. One explained that the proprietors believed that insurance arrangements would compromise the paper: it might be encouraged to settle and/or apologize when in fact the story was correct and it would be appropriate to contest any libel action. Two of these respondents said their paper kept a 'libel reserve fighting fund', in one case of £20,000 and in the other of £45,000 (out of which latter sum £3,500 to £4,000 was paid annually for legal fees and small settlements). Our sample suggested that it is relatively uncommon for a local paper (or group) not to take out libel insurance, but the NMIS has the impression that about 40 per cent of papers prefer to bear their own risk.

The Newspapers Mutual Insurance Society Ltd is a non-profit-making organization formed in 1932. Its board is composed of newspaper editors and directors; two solicitors usually attend board meetings. The Society is managed by Willis Coroon. It covers about seventy groups and 2,500 titles. Other prominent insurers include Lloyd's syndicates, Cigna, and the Sun Alliance.

A majority of the editors whose papers do take out insurance (fourteen out of twenty-three) said that the policy dictated which firm of solicitors was used, Oswald Hickson, Collier and Co., while in other cases the paper could choose from a list of about five 'approved' firms. A particular firm is in principle dictated by the NMIS policy, but not by the Lloyd's syndicate policy we examined. However, in practice even under the NMIS insurance arrangements a paper would usually be free to negotiate the choice of another solicitor. Conversely, other policies might in certain cases require the insured paper to consult a particular firm of solicitors. It is standard for policies to require the newspaper to notify the insurer's solicitors as soon as possible of any claim or circumstances likely to give rise to a claim. The insurers may require it to offer and/or publish an apology in the form settled by them. Further, the NMIS and other insurers are entitled through their solicitors to take over the defence of any libel action, which they may determine whether to compromise or fight. Moreover, one editor said in interview that it would always be sensible to consult the insurers' solicitors before publication of a sensitive story in order to avoid the risk of a conclusion that the editor had been reckless. But pre-publication consultation is not usually required under any of the insurance policies we examined. We were told that the NMIS would only refuse to pay if there had been a breach of contract, for example, if the paper failed to notify it of a claim in good time. The solicitor emphasized that the vast majority of claims—he thought about 95 per cent—arose from stories about which his firm had not been consulted prior to publication. Another insurer's representative told us that it was unheard of in her experience to require a regional paper to submit copy before publication, but this was quite common in contrast with some libel-risky periodicals. In their case there was more time before publication for a story to be checked.

Despite these provisions, no fewer than thireen editors (out of the twenty who replied to the question) denied that insurers exercised any significant influence over the handling of libel actions or applied pressure to settle when the newspaper would have preferred to fight. One said there was never any disagreement and matters were settled by an exchange of views. On the other hand, two said pressure was applied. One of them had changed his insurance policy as a result. Insurers' representatives and the solicitor both confirmed that disagreement about the handling of a claim was very rare indeed. The solicitor would act for both the newspaper and the insurers as two separate clients, consulting both of them at each stage. This would be done by fax or telephone; only exceptionally would a formal meeting be held.

We asked how much the newspaper (group) paid by way of insurance premium and whether the costs of its policy had increased much over the last five years. Only a minority of editors replied to these questions: some said they did not know. The answers suggested that annual premiums range from £1,089 to

£46,600, the latter being the sum paid for cover of a large group (five paid-for papers and thirty free weeklies). Four papers reported premiums at the £2,000 level, while at the other end three (including the large group already referred to) mentioned figures of £17,000 or more. One editor said the premium had increased from £16,900 in 1990–1 to £41,000 in 1994–5. But his cover had doubled to £500,000 in that period, so it would in his view be wrong to infer much from the increase. While two editors said their premiums had not increased much over the last five years, rather more said they had. For instance, one reported a 45 per cent increase over the previous year, while another said his premium had increased from £8,000 to £20,000. Others referred to 'considerable' or 'enormous' increases. The NMIS said premiums ranged from £375 to £60,000, and a similar range was quoted by a representative from one of the Lloyd's syndicates.

Insurance policies stipulate a ceiling on the amount which the insured paper may recover for payments it makes by way of damages or settlement and legal costs. According to the replies to our questionnaire, for smaller papers a ceiling of £100,000 is common, while the larger groups take out cover for about £500,000. The NMIS reported a range of cover from £30,000 to £750,000, though a cover of £1,000,000 has been arranged. Lloyd's appears to cover larger sums; a representative suggested that cover of £1 million was quite common, while a large regional group might take out insurance for up to about £5 million. Equally the newspaper is required by the policy to bear the first part of the loss itself, the 'excess'. Typically this is £5,000 or £10,000, but a few editors mentioned a much higher sum, £50,000, or in one case £75,000. As one editor put it in interview, this means 'that the company is covered for the extreme examples'. The NMIS thought the typical excess was about £1,000, but did not deny that in some cases it was much higher. We even heard of an excess of £100,000. The figures quoted by the Lloyd's syndicate were very similar.

Our final question concerned the overall annual costs of libel— including insurance premium, legal fees, and settlement/

damages—for the paper. There was a poor response to the question, over a third of editors giving no answer at all.

Table 8. *Broad estimate of how much libel costs your paper annually in terms of insurance premium, legal costs, settlements*

Less than £5K	10
£5K–£10K	4
£10K–£35K	3
Over £35K	6

At the lower end estimated costs of about £3,000 were the most common, while the highest figures were about £80,000 (a single paper) and about £72,000 (for a large group of papers which had a premium of over £46,000 and incurred average annual costs of about £25,000). One respondent at the high-cost end was not insured, but said the estimated annual cost of about £36,000 was distorted by one particular case which had cost his paper in the region of £100,000.

We also asked whether overall costs had risen appreciably in the last five years. The response to this question was very poor, only a small majority, five to three, saying that they had. This is surprising since it is fairly clear that there has been a significant increase in the insurance premium, which constitutes a major element in total costs.

Of course, in absolute terms these sums may seem trifling compared to the comparable libel expenditure of national newspapers and broadcasters (so far as we have been able to get figures). Nevertheless, they may be very significant for the regional press. This emerged very clearly from the interviews we conducted. Editors agreed that annual expenditure of about £50,000 on libel would be significant; it represented the salaries of two or three senior journalists. Another said it would amount to about 10 per cent of his variable costs and 'certainly £50,000 as a one off item of expenditure is really running into very major proportions'. He added that no editor could afford to take lightly a mistake that might cost thousands. A third editor (of a Sunday paper) said that two such settlements would wipe out the whole of his promotions budget or a quarter of his staff. In most cases a payment or settlement of this size would be recovered under the insurance policy, but this would not be the case where there was a large excess, or alternatively the newspaper had behaved recklessly or failed to disclose some important fact, so invalidating the insurance arrangements.

Conclusion

There are clearly substantial differences in the overall impact of defamation law on the regional press from that we found in other branches of the media, most particularly the national press. First, we are impressed by the editors' personal concern with libel matters, whether with regard to the decision to publish a story or in the investigation of complaints. This is obviously connected with the almost universal absence of in-house lawyers. Editors almost invariably resolve complaints in a personal and informal way by letter or over the telephone. A second conclusion is that editors are concerned at the potentially significant financial consequences of libel proceedings, and for that reason feel vulnerable. It does seem that they are reluctant to cover stories, unless they are absolutely sure that a plea of justification will be upheld in court. No editor admitted that sometimes a risk would be run simply because the story was a good one or might appear in a rival publication. A third point is that this caution may be reinforced by the editor's sensitivity to local opinion and a reluctance to lower his paper's standing in the community.

5

Broadcasting

Introduction

Obviously there are important legal and practical differences
between the positions of newspapers and the broadcasting media.
As far as the law is concerned, it must be remembered that the
latter are relatively tightly regulated, in that, first, a licence must
be granted before a commercial broadcaster, whether of radio or
television, is free to operate; secondly, broadcasting legislation[1]
imposes a number of detailed programme requirements; and
thirdly (at the time of writing), the Broadcasting Complaints
Commission controls, among other matters, the fairness of
programmes.[2] Equally, the BBC operates under a Charter and an
Agreement, which impose broadly similar programme standards
to those governing private channels and stations; further, it is also
subject to the control of the Broadcasting Complaints Commission
(BCC) in the same way as private radio and television. Broadcasters therefore operate in a culture of control and regulation, far
removed from that found in the press, whether national or
regional.

An important practical difference is that many programmes,

---

[1] Broadcasting Act 1990, as amended by the Broadcasting Act 1996.

[2] The Broadcasting Act 1996 merged the Broadcasting Complaints Commission,
which has exercised jurisdiction over complaints of unfairness and infringement of
privacy, with the Broadcasting Standards Council, which monitored programmes
from the perspective of violence, sexual explicitness, and bad language. It is
contemplated that this will take effect at some stage in 1997.

for example, documentaries and drama, are made several months before transmission, while it is relatively unusual for an item in a newspaper to be in preparation for more than a few weeks. This longer gestation period enables lawyers to monitor the programme as it is researched and made in order to remove libel and other legal risks. But clearly this point does not apply to news and other live programmes, where it may be at least as difficult to obviate legal risks as it is for newspapers printed only a few hours before distribution. A second difference is that television has a simultaneous visual and verbal impact on viewers, which may create greater risks of 'unintentional defamation', through the accidental pictorial association of the plaintiff with commentary which (he alleges) defames him, albeit wholly unintentionally. For example, a documentary on teenage drug abuse which shows film of boys leaving school might quite accidentally defame them by suggesting that they were parties to this abuse or had violated the drugs legislation.[3] More generally, it may be easier for listeners and viewers to ascribe a defamatory meaning to remarks made on radio and television, in that they do not have exactly the same opportunity to re-examine them as readers have with items in a newspaper or book. (They may however acquire a tape of the broadcast; broadcasters are legally required to keep such tapes for certain periods to enable the regulatory bodies to monitor their programmes.)

For these reasons we anticipated that there might be significant differences in the impact of defamation law on the broadcasting media from that found in the case of the newspaper industry. We also wanted to discover whether there are significant differences between radio and television in this context. Another question was whether there are differences between the impact of this area of law on broadcasters transmitting their own programmes and on those broadcasters which in effect act as publishers, showing programmes made by independent producers; a third issue was the variety of insurance arrangements.

---

[3] See the discussion of this issue in Ch. 1.

Research Methods

We sent a short questionnaire to lawyers working for the BBC and for a small number of commercial terrestrial broadcasters. We also conducted extensive series of interviews with some lawyers working for the BBC and a few of the private channels. For others we conducted single, isolated interviews. We talked in addition to a number of senior editorial staff, programme producers in a variety of departments, investigative journalists, and solicitors in private practice who work on a regular basis for Channel 3 licensees. However, no satellite or cable company was involved in the research, largely conducted in 1994. The decision not to involve these companies and their lawyers was to some extent taken for reasons of time, but also because for the most part they had only begun to broadcast in 1993–4 and at the time (and indeed now) there had been nothing to suggest they had any significant involvement with this area of law.

The response to the questionnaires was uniformly helpful. In addition, the series of interviews gave us a comprehensive picture of the day-to-day impact of defamation on the working life of in-house legal staff; they were conducted over an extensive period of two to three months for each broadcasting institution during the first half of 1994, and focused on their work at that time. One particularly helpful interview was given by a lawyer who had worked for a former Channel 3 licensee, now an independent producer; another lawyer was only able to give statistical evidence for 1993, as distinct from the five-year period 1988–93, since his company had only started broadcasting on 1 January 1993. These differences, however, have not prevented us from building a coherent picture.

Statistical Information

In this section we summarize some of the responses to the questionnaire. As this was sent to only six companies, their responses are not presented in tabular form. We asked them first about the number of writs issued in the five year period, 1988–93. The answers from the commercial channels ranged from one (for the new post-1993 licensee) to forty-two; the BBC chose to give figures for the five years from 1990–5, when it received eighty writs. (It must of course be borne in mind that the BBC has two television channels, five national radio channels, and a large number of local radio stations.) In contrast, none of these respondents fought more than three libel cases in court in the United Kingdom during the relevant period. The majority of claims are settled, sometimes with an apology which is either broadcast or read in open court. Compensation, or more usually compensation plus costs, is generally paid. However, two company lawyers said that it would be unusual for an apology to be offered once a writ has been issued, at any rate until the case is settled. One lawyer added that perhaps ten times a year an apology, sometimes with a substantial payment, will be offered and accepted, even before a writ has been issued. (There is further discussion of the procedure for dealing with claims later in the Chapter.)

We asked respondents to give an estimate of the number of letters before action, or other serious threats of libel proceedings, they received annually. The answers here varied significantly, one commercial company giving an overall figure of seventy, two others about thirty to forty, while a fourth said it received only about five serious threats a year. The majority of letters and faxes came from solicitors, while individuals and organizations tended more to complain about general unfairness to the Broadcasting Complaints Commission (BCC) or the BBC Programme Complaints Unit established in January 1994.

Another set of questions concerned the number and organization of in-house legal staff, the proportion of their time devoted to libel work, and the extent to which outside lawyers were called on to give advice prior to transmission. The BBC has the largest number of legal staff, dividing them into four departments. Two of these are involved with libel. The Programme Legal Advice Department in 1994 had five members, one of whom worked part-time. Libel work occupied on average about 50 per cent of their time, though they found it hard to be precise about this, as libel checking was often mixed up with other legal work, particularly concerning complaints to the BCC. Broadly this department deals with pre-transmission matters, while the Litigation Department deals with complaints and writs. The head of this department, with six members engaged wholly or partly on libel matters, estimated that about 30 per cent of their time overall is devoted to libel.

The arrangements for commercial terrestrial television vary quite considerably. Channel 4 now has four in-house solicitors (three at the time of interview, early 1994), and it is estimated they spend between 40 and 60 per cent of their working week on libel-related issues. Some Channel 3 licensees employ one or two in-house lawyers to cover both pre-transmission clearance and complaints, etc., though one company said it employed an outside lawyer to give advice on a particularly contentious series. Each of them said that libel work took up about half his time or, if anything, slightly more than that. In contrast, some licensees employ a London firm of solicitors on a retainer basis for vetting programmes, as well as for dealing with other legal matters. Whatever the arrangements, it is apparently rare for broadcasters to consult the Bar on the libel risks of a particular programme before transmission: a standard answer was that this happened about four or five times a year, though one lawyer said he had never sought counsel's opinion in these circumstances. Broadly, the proportion of time devoted to libel matters and the extent to which barristers are asked for an opinion are in line with what we discovered with regard to the national press, confirming both the significance of this area of law and the degree to which it is generally handled inside the institution itself.

Pre-transmission Procedures

These vary considerably according to the character of the programme. Some particularly contentious programmes, e.g.,

Panorama, World in Action, The Cook Report, Dispatches, will frequently entail the involvement of lawyers at an early stage. That may be two or three weeks, or on occasion even a few months before the anticipated date of transmission. The Channel 4 lawyers said it was quite common for them to be involved before a programme was commissioned by an editor. They would give advice about the legal risks attached to the proposal, though it would be for the editor to decide whether to proceed with the commission. A BBC lawyer intimated that he was generally consulted between two weeks and two months before a programme such as *Panorama* or *Watchdog* was due to go out. Other lawyers referred to earlier consultation on general programme ideas and libel risks, and the sort of evidence which must be obtained to substantiate the allegations the programme was likely to make. As the date for transmission draws near, lawyers may be more closely involved, reading scripts, viewing draft editions of the programme, and talking to producers and editors.

On the other hand, legal advice is constantly sought with regard to news bulletins and live programmes which cannot be monitored before transmission. The BBC operates a duty rota, with each lawyer taking turns to staff a 'hot-line' advisory service. This was set up to deal with news bulletins, but now provides a comprehensive service. The duty lawyer will expect to be telephoned about forty to fifty times on these days, with a variety of questions relating to libel, contempt, and other issues. Calls come from editors, but more often from the journalist working on the particular item. When appropriate he will be advised to inform his editor or other senior person of the libel risk.

Quite apart from the BBC 'hot-line', it is clear that a lot of legal advice, both inside the BBC and in the private sector, is given over the telephone. Indeed, the Head of the BBC Programme Legal Advice Department said that 'the majority of television checking [for libel] will be done over the telephone, it will be points arising in the programmes, rather than looking at the whole programme itself'. Much the same was said by a London solicitor who acts regularly for one of the Channel 3 licensees, who indicated that he only occasionally viewed a tape of a programme. The BBC lawyers will each view about four programmes a day on tape, so that about fifteen to twenty programmes overall will usually be monitored for libel risks in this way. That, however, compares with about sixty to seventy pieces of advice given each day on libel matters, as well as the assistance provided by the duty lawyer.

The decision to refer an item, or a whole programme, for legal advice is a matter for the editor. The legal staff rarely take the initiative, though this may happen when they become aware of a risk from informal discussion or through their general continuing relationship with the programme team. Both lawyers and editors see their relationship as broadly co-operative. Put simply, the former regard their role as that of enabling the programme to go out with as little alteration as possible to safeguard it from significant libel (and other legal) risks. As one programme-maker put it, 'the lawyers are enablers—people think the lawyer is getting to get in the way and not let you say things. That is not true. . . . They will often help you to find another word.' One experienced lawyer in the commercial sector emphasized that his relationship with the programme editors and journalists was a 'collaborative developing process'. The final version of the programme would be agreed: 'so it's unlike seeing newspaper copy and then cutting it, you are working with them all the way through'. But he agreed that the same could not be said of news bulletins, where the lawyer sometimes had to act more decisively and insist on an item's rewording or deletion.

In a co-operative context, it might be misleading to expect that either the lawyer or the editor would necessarily have the last word. But both lawyers and editors said that ultimately the latter took the decision if agreement was not reached whether an item should be dropped or changed. Legal *advice* was just that. One lawyer in the private sector did say his advice had always been taken, though he was sure that of others had been disregarded! Perhaps he had in mind the London solicitor who modestly admitted: 'In general they take the advice, sometimes, but not always. One makes a suggestion as to a change and we have a bargaining process frankly.'

Sometimes disagreements about whether it is worth running the risk of legal proceedings are referred higher up in the institution. Again this most frequently occurs in the context of programmes such as *World in Action* or *Panorama*, which have a lengthy gestation period, and which can be held over for further investigation if the evidence appears too weak at the time to justify the allegations. The BBC procedure is to refer the matter up the hierarchy. The Controller of Editorial Policy would expect to be informed about particularly controversial programmes, and hence the possibility of legal proceedings, and the matter might then be discussed with the Managing Director of the relevant directorate and the Legal Adviser. They would then take the decision whether the item should go out in its present form. On very rare occasions a programme with very serious libel risks has been referred to the Director-General, but never to the Board of Management as a whole. On the other hand, the Legal Adviser might report these issues to the Board and answer questions there about his decisions.

Similar procedures apply in the private broadcasting sector. A disagreement whether to accept legal advice may be referred to the Head of Legal Affairs or to the Company Secretary, but very rarely, it seems, to the full Board (which might be much more concerned with general libel and other litigation costs, as discussed below). One lawyer thought it appropriate to refer to the Managing Director as a referee; he might look at two or three libel matters a year, when he would take account of both the legal and commercial aspects before deciding whether the particular item should go out. In another, larger company the Head of Legal Affairs said he was consulted about once a month, and might refer about half these matters to the full Board. But he doubted whether it would really be practicable to discuss pre-transmission libel difficulties at its scheduled meetings. He would discuss hard cases with the Finance Director, who takes Board responsibility for legal affairs.

Self-censorship by Journalists?

Many journalists and some lawyers stressed that there was much self-censorship by journalists well before a request for legal help was made. Political and documentary editors and journalists are clearly well versed in the general principles of defamation law, and we found that they were familiar with the implications of the fundamental point that it is for the defendant to prove the truth of the story. One experienced producer said: 'Often it doesn't even get to the lawyer because we have decided that even though we believe that person is for instance a drug runner, we do not have the evidence at the moment to say so.' He emphasized that it was always a matter at that stage of deciding whether a story was potentially strong enough to justify the time and money which would be incurred in gathering sufficient evidence to broadcast it. In one case, a successful search had been made for several months to find a witness to an atrocity. That had cost the company nearly £20,000. Significantly, he added that less important items would have been killed off after a couple of weeks if it appeared difficult to find adequate evidence.

A similar impression was given by another producer, who had also worked for a number of years for a leading Sunday newspaper. In his view allegations were constantly toned down or deleted because television journalists became aware, or were advised, that they could not be substantiated. Indeed, he thought that broadcasting institutions were in one respect more vulnerable than newspapers: in practice defamatory allegations had to be substantiated by witnesses willing to appear on screen. He said: 'so I'm leaping higher probative hurdles just in order to fulfil the technical requirements of television programmes i.e., pictures and so on.' A lawyer working for another company was sure that there were stories which never reached him. The production team would have decided that it would not be able to substantiate them. Sometimes it would realize that the issue was not even worth investigation for that reason.

Problematic Programmes and Items

Current affairs programmes and documentaries obviously pose
libel risks. Particular programmes within this genre such as
Panorama, *World in Action*, *The Big Story*, and *Dispatches*, were
constantly mentioned as those which were more or less automatically previewed by lawyers to remove, or reduce the scale of,
these dangers. Other similarly risky categories are general
investigative programmes, e.g., *The Cook Report*, and consumer
affairs programmes, e.g., *Watchdog*. One lawyer wrote in reply to
the questionnaire: 'By far the most important source of libel
difficulties are programmes which may loosely be described as
consumer-type programmes. News broadcasts and, above all else,
current affairs programmes have presented . . . considerable libel
problems but nothing like as much as consumer-type programmes.' The BBC seemed very concerned with regional news
and current-affairs items, where perhaps monitoring (by local
journalists) is less attentive to legal difficulties than it is in the case
of national news items.

Perhaps more surprising was the inclusion of dramas and docu-
dramas in the danger category. In particular they create a risk of
an 'unintentional' or accidental defamation through the association of real-life figures, such as politicians, with the characters in
the drama. The dangers are most acute when the fictional
documentary is based on an actual recent event, e.g., the
Falklands War or the sexual affairs of ministers or MPs. It is then
quite easy for someone to claim that viewers might understand
the fictional character to represent him, and therefore that he was
defamed by the drama. The general problem of unintentional
defamation is discussed later.

Other items mentioned as risky were City and financial-affairs
programmes, and anything to do with boxing. Generally sports
and arts programmes were at the lower end of the scale. The
lawyers for Channel 4 emphasized that, although in principle all
types of item and programme were subject to libel checking,

certain types of programme, in particular investigative current-affairs items, were given particular scrutiny.

How Often did the Lawyer Intervene and on What Grounds?

These issues go to the heart of the alleged chilling effect of libel law: are stories of real public interest killed or significantly amended and on what grounds? We asked the lawyers to keep a log of their work over fortnightly periods to estimate how often they advised the amendment or deletion of an item, or more radically an alteration to the emphasis, or the dropping, of an entire programme. Unfortunately, their answers were imprecise. One BBC lawyer who had checked about twelve to fifteen programmes a day estimated he had advised about twelve changes in various programmes over the previous fortnight (out of a total of about 100, that is, in about 8 per cent). A Channel 4 lawyer reported about a range of three to four to six to seven significant interventions over fortnightly periods, during the course of which he normally checked about twelve to fifteen programmes. None of the lawyers who worked in the commercial sector admitted that any programme had been entirely dropped because of fear of libel proceedings, though the BBC said that this did happen, albeit infrequently. However, it was often the case that *particular items* in news bulletins had been dropped. The reply to one questionnaire estimated that fewer than 10 per cent of programmes suffered significant amendment or the dropping of an item, an answer which is in line with the evidence given to us in interview.

However, every respondent admitted that significant amendments were made—to tone down the language, remove particular shots which carried a risk of unintentional defamation, or delete an item or film passage containing unprovable allegations. One lawyer in the commercial broadcasting sector thought that he recommended very significant changes to the character of a programme at least once a month. Countless examples were given, of which we can only mention a few drawn from a variety of companies to give a flavour of the practical impact of libel law:

There were three or four amendments to a documentary about a series of hospital murders to remove possible allegations about the responsibility of various public employees. The lawyer had spent several hours looking at scripts and viewing versions of the programme.

Allegations in a regional television programme concerning ill-treatment and beatings by police officers in police cells after arrest were removed in view of insufficient evidence.

A major current affairs programme about paedophilia was restructured to remove suggestions that prominent figures colluded in a cover-up. Although the deletion involved only three or four minutes out of a 55 minute programme, it was substantial in character.

An item on *Newsnight* on the negligent management of an unlicensed children's home was deleted, because of insufficient evidence, the probable unreliability of the crucial witness, and awareness that the potential plaintiff had the resources to sue.

A *Today* programme item on a religious sect was dropped because it was advised allegations made by only two or three of its former members concerning abuse by its leaders would not stand up against evidence from its supporters.

Allegations about the involvement of a professional person in a prominent contract killing were removed. Although there was some evidence to support the allegations, the lawyer advised the witnesses would be too untrustworthy and tainted to substantiate them in court. The programme went out in a considerably bowdlerized form.

These are examples of some of the more significant interventions mentioned to us in interview. Perhaps more typical on a daily basis are suggestions to tone down the language or remove a particular camera shot. Both lawyers and editors stressed the importance of being able to defend every possible meaning, since it could not be assumed that listeners and viewers would understand a story or remark in the sense intended by the producer.[4]

What emerged from our research was the vital importance of evidence substantial enough to uphold the allegations. A senior BBC lawyer said there 'must be an overwhelming preponderance of facts'. On the other hand, someone working for a commercial company thought that often before transmission less supporting material was in practice required than there would be in the courtroom. That would suggest that sometimes broadcasters, like national newspapers, are prepared to take a gamble—though his was an isolated remark. What is clear is that the quality of the evidence required to justify a decision to go ahead will vary according to the nature of the allegations and the character of the programme. Witnesses with a criminal record or with a history of mental illness will be regarded as too unreliable to justify allegations, for instance, of police brutality or of abuse in a children's home or mental hospital. For similar reasons, two lawyers said it is difficult to make programmes about terrorism— witnesses are reluctant to appear on-screen and refuse to undertake to appear should proceedings be launched.

In certain circumstances, the lawyer will be concerned about the potential number of witnesses. One example of this was given above. The producers of a consumer programme such as *Watchdog* are less likely to be deterred if they can rely on a large number of consumers to support the complaints aired in the programme. In other cases, the lawyer may insist on getting documentary evidence to support the evidence of witnesses prepared to talk on camera, but it is unusual to require signed affidavits to guarantee their veracity. That step is simply not practical when the broadcast is to be transmitted, if at all, within a

---

[4] See the decision of the Court of Appeal in *Gillick v. BBC*, *The Times*, 20 Oct. 1995, where the CA held by a majority that the words used in a discussion programme could bear the meaning that the plaintiff was responsible for two pregnant girls' suicide after her (temporarily successful) campaign to inhibit the provision of contraceptive advice to girls under 16.

few hours. Original documents, e.g., minutes of a meeting where the truth of the allegations has been accepted, or the evidence of a witness prepared to talk on the programme, are in practice regarded as the best forms of supporting evidence. In contrast lawyers are less impressed when a witness wants to be 'off the record' or only consents to be interviewed with his face blanked out.

Although the amount and quality of evidence are the most important factor in determining whether to advise changes, it is not the only one. Other considerations are the likelihood of an action and the complainant's financial resources. Sometimes a broadcaster may be surprised by the plaintiff's resources, as apparently happened with the BBC when it made defamatory allegations about Dr Gee in *That's Life* without realizing that he was sufficiently wealthy to sustain legal proceedings. There is no doubt that broadcasters are more hesitant when they know from experience that the potential plaintiff has the capacity to sue. They are particularly cautious about stories which might implicate persons with an established litigation record. In this context there was frequent mention of the Police Federation, Rechem, British Nuclear Fuels, and the late Robert Maxwell.

One phenomenon we found particularly striking is the extent to which producers of some current-affairs and consumer programmes may come under pressure from potential plaintiffs *before* their transmission. One producer described how she is regularly bombarded with letters and faxes, sometimes three or four times a day, challenging her research and explicitly threatening libel proceedings if defamatory allegations are made. These are time-consuming and annoying to deal with, though they sometimes provide fresh information which can be incorporated in the programme to its benefit. Broadcasters are perhaps more vulnerable than newspapers or book publishers to this pressure, because they run the risk that the Broadcasting Complaints Commission will find unfair treatment if the allegations have not been put to the person concerned. So he will almost always know that a programme is being made and often quite a lot about its contents. The BBC for instance came under huge pressure from Robert Maxwell in the three or four weeks before it transmitted the *Panorama* programme about him shortly before his death in 1991. He was repeatedly on the telephone trying to discover exactly what allegations would be made against him, though apparently he declined an invitation to be interviewed for the programme.

Although lawyers admitted that their advice would be affected if they thought there was a possibility that the particular broadcast might lead to high damages and costs, they vigorously denied that it would be affected by the *general* costs of libel, say, over the previous months or year. In other words, as one lawyer put it, 'I would never say we have been blistered on two or three occasions and therefore we are going to be very careful now.' A very senior producer in the commercial sector said that she had never experienced any constraint in programme-making from general financial factors, or a directive from the Board (but she was sure it sometimes affected the settlement process).

The Problem of Unintentional Defamation

All the lawyers and many of the producers emphasized the difficulties of avoiding liability for what is often described as 'unintentional defamation'. As already explained,[5] television broadcasters are particularly vulnerable to this risk, because a camera shot may quite inadvertently suggest that some passer-by is implicated in a story about, say, drugs or police malpractice, when he has nothing at all to do with it. Alternatively, the name of a real person or company might be accidentally used in a series or drama which purports, of course, to be about wholly fictitious events. This second variety of 'unintentional defamation' may, of course, also affect book and periodical publishers, and to some extent the press. So far as broadcasters are concerned, it is obviated to some extent by a process known as 'negative

[5] See Ch. 1, p. 7, and this Ch. p. 101.

checking' under which relevant street and professional directories, and the Companies Register, are checked to see whether someone actually exists with the name used in the programme, with a similar address and other details to that of the relevant character. This work is done either in-house or on a freelance basis. The BBC lawyers described the process very fully. For the last few years, it has employed two people, one full-time and one half-time, for this purpose: 'the negative checking section of the reference library . . . spends [its] whole life running through lists of fictitious characters and comparing them with lists of doctors, dentists, policemen,[6] butchers in Blackburn and things like that'. The procedure would lead to about four or five references a week to the legal department. The system had only failed to safeguard the BBC on a handful of occasions, and the Head of the Programme Legal Advice Department thought the staff salaries were amply met by the savings in defamation settlements and costs. A commercial company lawyer agreed that the procedure was necessary, albeit it was fallible; about once every two years he received a complaint of inadvertent defamation of this type. Another procedure is for the television company to register a shell company at Companies House to ensure that no actual company trades under that time while the programme is made!

It is less easy to avoid liability for the accidental inclusion of the plaintiff in a camera shot. An instance was given of film which quite inadvertently contained a shot of the premises of one company when it was intended to suggest that another company, trading on the same industrial estate, had been incompetent. The former company complained and the broadcaster apologized and paid its costs. This seemed a relatively common incident; one BBC lawyer recalled about half a dozen instances over the previous year or so, two of which had led to the payment of compensation. Risks can be reduced by careful scrutiny of all versions of the programme, including the final film and its title

---

[6] For instance, the names of police officers mentioned in the scripts for *Inspector Morse* are checked with the Thames Valley police.

sequence. There is great reluctance to use old film in a documentary or current affairs programme, on, for example, drug abuse or under-age gambling, in case it involves wholly innocent people. ITN, we were told, uses fresh footage whenever possible to illustrate a story.

Libel and the Broadcasting Complaints Commission

One point frequently made was that broadcasters are subject to a regulatory system which itself induces a degree of circumspection not found in the newspaper industry. An unwarranted remark, let alone a distorted programme, may lead to either a libel writ or a complaint to the Broadcasting Complaints Commission (to be merged in 1997 with the Standards Council into the Broadcasting Standards Commission), which has sometimes seen itself as a 'poor-man's libel court'.[7] The producers of investigative and consumer programmes have been alive to the possibility that a complaint of unfair or unjust treatment may be made to the BCC after transmission.

One anxiety is that a complaint to the Commission may be used as a 'dry run' for subsequent defamation proceedings. Neither the BCC, nor the new Standards Commission, has any duty to reject complaints because it considers that they could be the subject of a legal remedy, so it is perfectly possible for a complainant to use the Commission to gather evidence for subsequent libel proceedings. One BBC lawyer said that in three cases a writ had followed a complaint, while others thought the anxiety was a little exaggerated. Complaints to the Commission were more likely to be brought by pressure groups which would be unable to bring a libel action or by individuals unable to afford legal proceedings.

On the other hand, some commercial television lawyers argued that a complaint to the BCC had increasingly been used as a rehearsal for a libel action. On one view, the complainant's objective is not so much to gather evidence for this action as to see

---

[7] See its Annual Report for 1993, 1993 HC 806, para. 4.

what meaning it gives to the allegations in the programme: 'they are using the BCC who are ordinary people by and large as a trial run for the jury and it's largely on meaning rather than on evidence'. Other lawyers said they frequently found that an initial letter contemplating or threatening libel proceedings was soon followed by notice from the Commission of a complaint about the programme from the same person; the significance of this experience is that they became cautious in dealing with the complaint in case any information they supplied was used to support legal proceedings. One lawyer said that an adverse ruling by the Commission on the fairness of a programme had been successfully used to put pressure on the broadcaster to settle a libel action.

The impact of the alternative avenue of recourse to the Commission is hard to evaluate without further research. But it seems likely that the prospect of a complaint reinforces the care which broadcasters and their lawyers take to avoid libel proceedings; moreover, a Commission finding, or evidence acquired during its investigation, may make it easier to induce the broadcaster to settle libel proceedings. We now turn to other issues involved in dealing with complaints and the settlement process.

Dealing with Complaints and Writs

The questionnaire raised a number of issues about the resolution of libel complaints. As already mentioned, the BBC has a separate Litigation Department with responsibility for dealing with post-transmission complaints and with legal proceedings. In fact, sometimes these complaints are handled, at least initially, by the lawyer in the Programme Legal Advice Department who had checked the programme before transmission. But other complaints, and all writs, are dealt with by lawyers in the Litigation Department. They are referred to the relevant programme editor who will investigate the accuracy of the allegations in conjunction with the lawyer. The latter then sends a letter to the complainant.

It is exceptional to seek counsel's advice before a writ has been issued.

Similar answers were given by lawyers for the private broadcasting companies (though they do not have a separate litigation department). The lawyer takes responsibility for checking the accuracy of the allegation and determining the appropriate course of procedure in consultation with the editor or the production company (where the broadcast publishes programmes made by an independent producer). However, unlike the BBC, private broadcasting companies are insured, so all serious complaints must be reported to the insurers and solicitors nominated under the insurance policy. (Insurance arrangements are discussed in the next section.) As with the BBC, it is rare to go out to counsel or external solicitors before a writ has been issued.

Replies to the questionnaires suggested that the majority of complaints were resolved without subsequent recourse to a writ or a complaint to one of the regulatory or complaints bodies. Some respondents simply said that the overwhelming majority of complaints were dealt with informally, while others put a figure of 60 or 70 per cent on this proportion. From the BBC it was said that about 30 per cent of the complaints were settled with a payment of money and (perhaps) an apology, even though no writ was served, while the outstanding 10 per cent or more of 'hard core' complaints led to writs. A lawyer for Channel 4 estimated that only 5 per cent of complaints were followed eventually by a writ, but 25 per cent of them led to a complaint to the ITC or one of the complaints bodies. One respondent thought it was harder for broadcasters to deal with a complaint by a formal apology, since the transmission of the latter interrupted the programme schedule and would require the consent of a number of people throughout her organization.

At some stage after the issue of a writ, when it has become clear that the claim will be seriously pursued, the broadcaster will have to decide whether to settle or fight. Producers and editors clearly often consider a case should be fought on principle; a settlement would in their view compromise their integrity when they are sure they have got the facts right. We came across some feeling about this with regard to one or two recent *causes célèbres*. On the other hand, the lawyers will be concerned with the prospects of winning the case. The decision of the BBC to fight the *Upjohn* action, unsuccessfully as it happened, was taken in the belief that it could be won on the evidence.[8] At the BBC the decision will be taken at a senior level. In exceptional cases this will involve consultation between the Legal Adviser, the Controller of Editorial Policy, and the Managing Director of, say, News and Current Affairs, but more usually the decision is taken formally by the Managing Director of the particular directorate or the particular Controller. At this stage the decision will be based on a mixture of financial and legal considerations: is there a chance the BBC will win, and what sort of damages and costs would be incurred if the case is lost?

One lawyer who had advised a Channel 3 licensee for a number of years stressed the financial gamble his client took when it decided for reasons of principle to fight a case. There were difficult decisions at each stage in the procedure whether to settle or to make a payment into court.[9] He was sure that on a couple of occasions cases had been settled for a mixture of financial and evidentiary reasons, when they might have been won. One factor which might play a part in private broadcasters' decisions to settle is pressure from the insurers. However, the majority of commercial television lawyers and editors thought this had never been a factor, but there was one interesting dissenter. He considered pressure had been applied in one or two cases at a late stage in the pre-trial proceedings: 'where one actually believes that one has the evidence to fight something but effectively for insurers it's more cost effective to settle rather than to fight, that's where it's very hard and that's happened once or twice.'

Some lawyers and broadcasters pointed out that a high

---

[8] Damages of £60,000 were awarded, while the costs incurred were about £1.5 million.

[9] For the implications of payments into court, see Ch. 1 above.

proportion of libel actions were dormant, though in this respect their experience did not seem significantly different from that of the national press. The Head of the BBC Litigation Department estimated that about 50 per cent of libel actions became dormant. She thought there was no single explanation for this phenomenon; in some cases the writ had been issued in the heat of the moment, while in others the plaintiff felt under pressure from his peers or business colleagues to take this step. As one BBC editor put it, '[w]e normally expect public figures when they have a programme that reveals unacceptable activities to issue us a writ, I mean that is what we expect them to do, if only to save face for themselves. But whether they then pursue it is a separate matter.'

In some cases, it is likely the plaintiff became inactive because he could not afford to continue with the proceedings. One journalist was sure that on occasion writs were issued, simply to deter the broadcasters and other parts of the media from following up a story or exploring other angles of the plaintiff's record. Certainly many cases go to sleep for one or two years, and are then unexpectedly revived. This happened in the action brought by Dr Skuse against Granada, which was based on a *World in Action* programme broadcast in 1985 concerning his medical evidence in the Birmingham Six trial. At various stages the case went to sleep, but eventually came to court in October 1994, nearly ten years after the alleged libel was committed.[10]

Insurance Arrangements and Financial Costs

The BBC has not taken out libel insurance for about fifteen years. It does, however, make provision for libel payments within its overall legal budget. This is not attached to particular programme or departmental budgets, for that would unduly constrain high-risk material, such as investigatory documentaries and consumer-affair programmes. The budget is controlled centrally by the

---

[10] The action was discontinued after opening speeches had been made and the case adjourned.

Legal Adviser, who will determine whether it is appropriate, say, to incur the costs of outside legal advice on a particular programme. Our evidence suggests that the 1994–5 budget allowed for £500,000 libel costs, excluding internal staff and other expenditure.

In contrast, each independent television licensee does take out an errors-and-omissions insurance policy. In the case of Channel 3 companies, this is a condition of access to the network. The policies cover all types of legal liability, ranging from libel to breach of confidence and copyright infringement, and cover liability for networked, regional, and acquired programmes. Only one independent company was prepared to mention the level of its annual premium (£250,000), though we gather another paid about £70,000 in 1993. However, a number of them volunteered that this cost had not risen appreciably over the last five years (a different impression from the one we received from regional newspaper editors and book publishers). One reason for this is that the insurance business, at least so far as broadcasting is concerned, is highly competitive, particularly after the entry of US insurance companies into the market in the last few years.

There is a variety of insurance and other contractual arrangements in respect of independent producers who are commissioned to make a programme for a Channel 3 licensee or Channel 4. Typically, they are covered by the broadcasting company's errors-and-omissions policy, in return for a warranty under which they are required to inform the broadcaster of any matter likely to give rise to libel, or other legal, liability. The broadcaster will indemnify the independent producer for any legal expenditure incurred by the latter. (The BBC enters into similar arrangements with its independent producers.) Alternatively, an independent producer may seek direct access to the ITV network without going through one of the regional licensees, and in that case it is required to make appropriate insurance arrangements under a tripartite contract made between it, a nominated Channel 3 licensee, and the ITV Network Centre. In that eventuality, it may take out an individual insurance policy for the particular series of programmes it wishes to have broadcast over the network or it may subscribe to a group policy covering a number of independent producers. We understand that premiums for a particular programme or series might range from £3–4,000 to £15,000 for a three part series which was thought particularly risky. Under the tripartite contract the nominated licensee has the responsibility for ensuring that the independent producer's insurance arrangements satisfy the contract's requirements and, further, that the broadcast does not contain any defamatory material (to the best of its belief).

Understandably, our respondents and interviewees were reluctant to give us an estimate of how much libel costs their company in a typical year. We did secure approximate figures from some Channel 3 licensees. They varied from over £1 million to £100,000. The former figure was regarded as disturbingly high by our interviewee. It was emphasized that annual expenditure could fluctuate wildly, depending on the size of one or two awards and legal costs. One answer said that insurance premiums had been increased significantly in the wake of the awards to Jeffrey Archer (£500,000) and Sonia Sutcliffe (£600,000).[11]

Broadcasters and Independent Producers

We did not find any evidence of difficulties arising from the relationship of 'publisher' broadcasters to their independent producers. All terrestrial television broadcasters, BBC and commercial, are now obliged to give at least 25 per cent of their time to independent productions, while some, for instance Channel 4 and Carlton, now act primarily as publishers of programmes which are either purchased or commissioned. In practice, the legal staff of the broadcaster vets the programme before transmission and deals with legal difficulties which may arise subsequently. The contractual and insurance arrangements

---

[11] This latter award was held unreasonable by the Court of Appeal, and subsequently a second jury awarded £60,000.

outlined in the previous section do not give rise to serious problems, though one lawyer admitted that her relationship with an independent producer is inevitably more formal than it is with in-house production staff. But another said that 'it's a system that doesn't cause friction.' The Channel 4 lawyers confirmed this impression, as did a lawyer who had worked for a licensee and now gave advice on a freelance basis to independent producers. There was agreement that generally independent producers tended to be more cautious about libel and other legal risks than the broadcasting company, largely because of their financial vulnerability. For the most part they employed lawyers only for contractual and property work, and left programme clearance and litigation to the broadcasting company.

The Different Position of Radio

We made no rigorous attempt to evaluate the position of radio in comparison with television. But the general view of our interviewees was that in practice it did not pose so many problems, and radio programmes attracted fewer writs. One BBC lawyer dissented from that view, and certainly we were given a number of examples in interview of how current-affairs and news items on radio gave rise to complaints. In particular, items are on occasion dropped from BBC radio news bulletins because of anticipated libel difficulties.

The Head of the Programme Legal Advice Department thought, however, that there were significant differences between the two media. First, radio attracts fewer listeners than television does viewers, so that a potential plaintiff may be less concerned by its output. Secondly, and perhaps more controversially, he thought television programmes were inherently riskier; they had less time for a detailed and balanced exposition of a political or financial issue, and were more inclined to sensationalism. Thirdly, radio lacks the risk of unintentional defamation associated with pictorial libel. This last point was made by two other lawyers who had worked for both radio and television.

Conclusions

The research confirmed our belief that there are significant differences between the impact of defamation law on the broadcasting and print media. The culture of control under which the former act is an important factor in inducing restraint; few newspaper journalists and lawyers mentioned the Press Complaints Commission in this context, while most of their peers in the broadcasting media were very alive to the possibility of a complaint to the BCC (now BSC). Clearly the long gestation period for current affairs programmes and documentaries gives time for thorough research. It was forcefully put to us by a journalist with substantial experience of both media that stories on the broadcasting media are better researched.

One lawyer and two producers thought the high costs of making television programmes also contributed to some initial caution in *investigating* risky stories. That is quite compatible with a willingness to broadcast allegations which are believed on good evidence to be true, despite the financial risks of this course. At that later stage there may be little difference between the attitudes of press and broadcasting lawyers (or journalists). Another point is that there is not the same competitive culture as there is in the national press. There is one principal news provider (ITN), rather than a number of players competing to present the fullest version of a sensational story.

We have found it much harder to evaluate another point put to us by a few interviewees. Broadcasting, they contended, is an essentially ephemeral medium, with much material passing the average viewer and listener by. Copies of a newspaper article, in contrast, may be circulated around a community, and any defamatory allegations will be mulled over and repeatedly discussed. There is much more risk, therefore, of a newspaper libel spreading and taking root than is the case with a similar story on radio or television. Finally, it can be said that, whether this is in fact the case or not, libel plaintiffs consider this to be the position. They are more sensitive, in short, to defamation in a newspaper article than on the audiovisual media. This argument may explain in part why there are almost certainly fewer writs against the latter than against the national press;[12] it is perhaps less persuasive, if it is designed to show that libel law poses significantly fewer problems for television than for the printed media. But the claim cannot easily be evaluated without a study of the attitudes of libel plaintiffs, a matter which was beyond the scope of our research.

[12] See the figures of cases set down for trial in Ch. 2

6

Book Publishers

Methodology and Statistical Data

As with the other media, a questionnaire specifically tailored to the working of the book trade was sent to a range of publishers in the spring of 1994. Sixteen responded, and may be regarded as broadly representative, in that they included both academic and purely commercial firms. The latter were evenly divided between those wholly or mainly publishing fiction and non-fiction. Several were part of major publishing conglomerates, and also included was one of the tiny remnant of individually-owned independent publishers which have shrunk in number from approximately 200 to fewer than ten since the end of the 1950s. Two university presses apart, virtually all the others were based in London.

The main areas covered by the questionnaires were (a) statistical information relating to the frequency and outcome of libel experience (ranging from letters before action through settlement to cases decided by jury verdict) over the preceding five years; (b) the procedures used to check manuscripts to minimize libel risks; and (c) financial and insurance arrangements. Not every respondent answered every question, but most questions were answered in full, although there was some reluctance (less, however, than we had expected) to give full details about insurance costs and 'libel budgets'. We discuss below the results of the questions, taking each category separately.

The responses highlighted certain issues and raised other interesting points, which were followed up by selective interviews. The choice of whom to interview was based largely on their declared willingness to discuss the broad issues further. Two editors, two in-house solicitors, and representatives of the two trade associations were interviewed at length. Interviews were also conducted with representatives of the Society of Authors and the Publishers Association. Additionally, a round-table discussion involving three other in-house solicitors and one law-firm solicitor with several publishing clients was arranged through the good offices of the Publishers Association.

Libel experience

Most notable in this respect was the huge variation revealed in the responses. Half the respondents (eight) had not received any libel writs during the preceding five years. One company, however, had received between twenty and thirty. Full trials were a rarity: only two respondents experienced them in that period. (One resulted in a verdict for the plaintiff, the other for the publisher.) Much more common were settlements, the great majority (nineteen) of which included payment of some monetary damages and costs; only three claims were simply withdrawn. For several reasons—not least because we have no details on the amount of legal costs—it is very difficult to identify an average for the expense of settlement. However, it would appear that both the median and the average figure are somewhere between £30,000 and £50,000.

The Peculiarities of the Publishing Industry

Book publishing is of course governed by the same uniform libel laws as all other media. However, there are certain characteristics of the trade that make it, in the views of all the respondents who raised the point, particularly vulnerable to the impact of those laws.

Foremost perhaps is the nature of the book itself. Unlike a newspaper, which tomorrow may line a cat-litter tray, or the even more ethereal character of broadcast transmissions, books have, and are designed to have, permanence. If reasonably popular, they will continually recirculate throughout the community via the public library system, and may well be reprinted over an extended period. Even works with smaller readerships will remain on purchasers' shelves for many years. Thus persons who believe themselves to have been libelled in a book fear that the damage will live on in a way that is not a danger with more ephemeral media. Hence they often seek permanent alteration or suppression of a book, which in any case would be impractical with other media. Overt censorship is thus a major problem in this field.

Secondly, with books it is both more difficult and much more expensive to respond to a complaint accepted by the publisher as valid other than by monetary compensation or withdrawing the book entirely. There is nothing analogous to a printed apology in tomorrow's or next week's edition of the same paper, or to a similar statement at the end of a television programme later in the same series—both of which may credibly be thought to reach roughly the same audience which had read or heard the original allegation. Only withdrawal of a book on a temporary basis, to enable insertion of an erratum slip containing an apology or excision of the offending passages is even remotely similar. Yet if the book has been released to the shops, that cannot be done quickly enough to achieve the same result as a prompt newspaper apology. And to recall a book once released can be a significant financial blow, owing both to the costs of re-issuance and to the loss of sales as marketing is delayed.

Finally, book publishers are subject to an uncertainty as to their liability which has no parallel in the other media. The limitation on liability for defamation has been fixed by statute at three years, half that normally governing most torts.[1] Liability runs from the date of commission of the act, which in this context means publication of the libel. For newspapers and broadcasters

---

[1] Limitation Act 1980, s. 4A. The Defamation Act 1996, s. 5 further reduces the limitation period to one year.

this is clear—the day of issue or transmission. For books, however, each sale constitutes a fresh 'publication' for purposes of the limitation period.

This legal rule has at least two consequences. Publishers operate a system known as 'backlisting'. Most books receive their heaviest marketing, and gain their greatest sales, in the first year after publication. Nonetheless they remain in print on the firm's backlist, and can be purchased either in shops or by direct request to the company's marketing department for some years afterwards. Hence so long as copies of a book remain available for sale, however infrequently sales may in fact occur, the threat of liability remains. Although this problem was cited to us as one of the perils of book publishing, it has probably diminished compared with twenty or thirty years ago: for economic reasons publishers now print fewer copies and concentrate more on trying to sell the full print run than was the practice then. Moreover, the absence of vertical integration in the industry means that publishers do not control the sale of their books, and thus must live with the possibility that, even if a book has gone out of print, odd copies may remain offered for sale by individual bookshops for a long time thereafter. Thus a letter of complaint and/or lawsuit relating to a long-forgotten book may pop up to hit them at almost any time.

In addition to these specifically legal factors, there are certain economic pressures that differentiate book publishing from newspapers and broadcasting companies.[2] Those media gain the great part of their income from advertising or, in the case of the BBC, direct subsidy through the licence fee. They are not dependent on the sale of a particular article—a daily newspaper produces over 300 editions annually, and save for some highly unusual scoop or fortuitous event, the number sold each day is very roughly constant. Book publishers by contrast survive on the success of a much more limited number of specific titles. Each of

---

[2] Independent production companies may be in an analogous position, however.

these has a profit margin: one can gain or lose money on a given book in a way which has no real analogy with one day's newspaper or television programme.

These margins are surprisingly tight. One respondent, a well-known publisher with a large list, estimated that a hardback sold at £14.99 would produce a profit for the publisher of 50p per copy—just over 3 per cent, after all overheads. Further, sales of 5,000 would put it in the bestseller class. Thus this publisher's profit on an unusually successful book would be £2,500.[3] It therefore requires very little by way of costs incurred by extra legal consultation, temporary withdrawal, delay preventing sale during the critically important run-up to Christmas—let alone a settlement including a money payment—to turn a successful venture into a loss-making one. The scale of potential loss from libel is therefore wildly out of proportion to the profit most books can be expected to generate. This produces a constant background pressure for caution, and under the circumstances it is surprising that rejections of proposals and deletions from manuscripts which have been accepted are not even more frequent and severe than currently is the case.

Taking Precautions

Once a manuscript has been received, the editor must determine whether it presents any significant risks in relation to libel and what measures should be taken to minimize those risks. Fewer than a third of our respondents employed in-house lawyers, but more than half had engaged solicitors or junior barristers to do a pre-publication reading of some manuscripts.[4] The extent to which lawyers are used in this way varies considerably. In two

---

[3] Other publishers with smaller lists reported higher per-volume profits. Nonetheless these figures make it obvious why small independent publishers have been largely driven out of the trade—and how devastating a big libel loss could be for those who remain.

[4] Estimates of the cost of libel reading varied considerably, from a standard £250 for one firm to £750–£1500 for another which uses junior barristers on the infrequent occasions when it requires a manuscript to be checked.

firms *all* non-fiction works were read, but most tended to be selective. Subject matter and genre seem to be the most important factors: biography and current affairs involving living persons are thought to require the most careful attention, as are certain classes of subject matter. These books involve the police, miscarriages of justice, sporting personalities, and books by certain investigative journalists. Very seldom is a novel regarded as sufficiently risky to require a libel reading, although one editor did write that 'We also refer fiction where our editors have reason to be concerned, particularly whenever authors have given us firm assurances that "I know he won't sue" '.

This process may have a significant effect on the book's final form. A majority of those who responded to this question reported that in at least 70 per cent of the instances where manuscripts have been vetted in this way, 'substantial' changes to the text had been recommended by the libel reader. We were unable to acquire a clear picture of the relations between readers and editors, though in the view of one editor a good lawyer-reader is one who knows the law, understands books, has an agile brain, and is pugnacious. This last characteristic may be particularly important, because the lawyer's job is to 'clear' the book—that is, suggest alterations that will leave it free from libel risk. This requires, as one former editor said, a lawyer 'who will sail as close to the wind as he can get away with'. Hence the need for toughness, for it is easy to err on the side of caution and, as it were, sterilize books to avoid problems.

Yet sterilization at least ensures that the manuscript sees the light of day, a result otherwise by no means guaranteed. Six of thirteen respondents had either not published or refused to acquire a manuscript for fear of libel. Not all were willing to describe the subjects covered, but those which were mentioned included books on boxing, a notorious police squad, and Robert Maxwell. In addition, one rejected manuscript concerned the author's alleged homosexual relationship with a pop star. Clearly not everything which is directly suppressed by libel is of equivalent value.

Two distinct aspects of libel were reported as the primary causes of difficulty. One is unintentional defamation, discussed in Chapter 1 (and in Chapter 5 specifically in relation to broadcasting). This is surprisingly common: more than half the respondents who received libel complaints had had at least one of this type. One example, now a matter of public record, concerned a novel about schooldays at Eton. The author, who took pains to avoid the problem, chose the names of his characters at random from the New York City telephone directory. Incredibly, the name he lit upon for a character depicted as a homosexual drug user turned out to be that of an Eton contemporary, although neither remembered the other. This comedy of errors had a sad ending for Faber and Faber, which had to pay damages (undisclosed) to a Mr Alex Wilbraham.[5] Short of maintaining a negative checking section like that of the BBC—not an economic proposition for a publisher—there is by definition nothing to be done to counter this risk.

The other problem was inability to prove the truth of libellous allegations. As was seen in Chapter 1, defendants carry the onus of proof in this respect and must meet the ordinary civil standard of balance of probabilities. In some instances this requirement may do no more than serve the useful function of ensuring that authors know their subject adequately, check their facts fully, do not rely unduly on hearsay or secondary materials, and generally do what is reasonably necessary to ensure the accuracy of their assertions. In the view of one in-house lawyer, 'much—though not all—of libel is the result of sloppy writing'.

However, the impact may also be much wider and less beneficial. The same respondent quickly added that the rest of libel is the problem of uncloaking cover-up. Even if an investigative writer can expose deliberate deception by powerful individuals or business organizations,[6] anything he writes may be

---

[5] See P. Marsh, 'What's in a Name? And Other Questions of Libel', *The Author*, Winter 1994, 147–8.

[6] As was reported in relation to the national press, politicians almost never sue in relation to matters concerning their conduct in office.

defamatory unless he can go further and positively establish the truth. The inability to do the latter may prevent publication of the former; in other words, merely stripping away lies can be dangerous. To assert, or indeed to imply, that someone has told lies is defamatory, and in practice (whatever the strict legal position may be) it is felt that to avoid liability it is necessary for a writer to go further than exposing deliberate falsehood: he must demonstrate the true version of events to an extent sufficient to stand a reasonable chance of convincing a jury. It is at this point that assertions are softened or disguised, passages deleted, and, in extreme cases, books are lost.

The publisher is subject here not only to the usual hazards of unreliable, out-of-jurisdiction, unsavoury (and therefore low-credibility) witnesses, missing documentation, and faulty memories after long delays, but to a problem that especially plagues investigative work in all media. This is the unwillingness of sources which are quite prepared to talk off the record to speak publicly and appear in court. Interviewees reported several instances in which major alterations to remove material they believed to be true were required because of the refusal of sources to co-operate in this way. English law creates the real possibility that, where neither the author nor his subject can incontrovertibly establish the truth, the former will fail through inability to shoulder the burden of demonstrating justification. It is here that the difference between English and American law[7] bites most sharply.

When Precautions Fail

Virtually every respondent had received at least one letter before action, i.e. a complaint, written either by the person concerned or, somewhat more commonly, by a solicitor. Several stated that the easiest to deal with were the genuine cases, in which people tended to be more concerned with having their names cleared—

[7] See Ch. 1, pp. 14–15.

which requires only an apology and correction—than with receiving damages. In such cases, an apology plus a small sum, often payable to charity, is sufficient to satisfy the complainant. Such changes may, however, mean significantly greater loss for the publisher. The costs of even temporary withdrawal for insertion of a correction are substantial, and may be supplemented by loss of sales momentum or opportunities in the critical pre-Christmas period. This experience is by no means uncommon: half the respondents (eight) had withdrawn one or more books because of threat of proceedings.

More severe losses may of course be incurred by agreed payments to plaintiffs. As noted earlier, we can only arrive at the rough estimate of £30–£50,000 for both the median and average settlements. However, at least two settlements of £50,000 plus costs of £25,000 were reported, as was one global figure of £100,000. As we have seen, even an all-inclusive loss of £10,000 would more than wipe out the profit expected from most books. What is most striking is the overwhelming incidence of payment (nineteen instances), as compared with withdrawal and simple apology combined (four). This may reflect the validity of the complaints; but in several instances it also embodies the view expressed by in-house lawyers for larger publishers that it is often better as a matter of strict economic calculation to pay a relatively small sum even to an 'unmeritorious' complainant to dispose of the matter at an early stage, rather than risk having to satisfy claims for his mounting legal costs if a settlement is reached closer to the courthouse door. This perceived necessity to pay off 'fortune hunters and ambulance chasers' is perhaps the aspect of libel which causes the most resentment.

In assessing the risk of libel posed by any manuscript, or deciding whether to meet a complainant's demands for alteration and/or damages as part of a negotiated settlement, book publishers are feeling their way blindly to a much greater degree than is true of other media. There appears to have been only one instance since the last War in which a libel action concerning a book has led to a judgment appearing in the official Law Reports, and that was the extraordinary case in which the publisher's conduct in repeating by advertisement the libellous allegations was held to justify the award of heavy punitive damages.[8] Just as the substantive law of libel has been developed overwhelmingly in relation to newspapers rather than books, there is virtually no history of jury behaviour where a book publisher is the defendant.[9] This imports an extreme degree of sheer guesswork into the settlement process, in which publishers seem far less willing even than other media to risk ending up in court. As one person put it, 'Publishing is a lottery in the first place, but it's a lot less of a lottery than the libel laws'—by which he meant primarily having to face a jury.

Insurance

Like all businesses, publishers may attempt to minimize financial risk by taking out insurance. Most do so, and whilst the details we were able to gain were not complete, they provide an interesting, and somewhat alarming, picture.

Since most publishers are now members of large corporate conglomerates, it is not surprising that virtually all are covered by a group policy. Whether this reflects deliberate corporate policy or is a reflection of a contraction in the market—a number of syndicates and companies which began offering libel insurance in the 1970s withdrew in the 1980s—could not be determined. What is most striking is the range of premiums paid—from a low of £8,000 to an estimate of between £65–100,000. That minimum figure is very much out of line with the others reported; it appears that a very rough median expenditure would be £20–40,000.

In addition, the great majority who answered this question reported that premiums have increased over the five-year period,

---

[8] *Cassell* v. *Broome* [1972] AC 1027.
[9] Count Tolstoy's pamphlet attacking Lord Aldington, which resulted in a jury award of £1.5 million and ended up in Strasbourg (see *Tolstoy Milosavsky* v. *United Kingdom* (1995) 20 EHRR 442) is entirely *sui generis*.

in some instances substantially. One company, for example, was being charged for the same cover nearly three times what it had paid in 1988. Moreover, the compulsory excess—the amount borne by the insured party before the insurer begins to pay—had *quintupled* in the same period. Other respondents reported similar, if not always so spectacular, trends. These increases seem quite unrelated to the libel record of the particular publisher. In one extreme instance, an independent publisher who had been free of claims for the preceding three years was faced with a percentage premium increase almost identical to the example cited above. He chose to proceed uninsured and run the risks—a notably bold response, and not one likely to be emulated by those operating within a large corporate structure.

Whilst insurers are reported as influencing, or in some cases conducting, settlement negotiations, their role seems to be limited to financial considerations. Certainly there was no mention of direct interference with editorial decisions. However, the 'double whammy' of increasing premiums and rising excess was cited as influencing the kinds of works that respondents would handle. We return to this point in the concluding section.

Relations between Publishers and Authors

Although publishers are the primary defendants in any action, the book's author, as originator of the libel, is as a matter of law liable as well. Authors are invariably listed as defendants when writs are issued. Since authors are neither limited companies nor, with rare exceptions, wealthy individuals, the publisher is inevitably the primary target of any plaintiff seeking financial compensation.[10] This vulnerability would make it both economically rational and—since the ultimate cause is the author's handiwork—equitable for the adverse consequences of libel to be shared between

---

[10] The publisher would of course also be the appropriate person for organizing deletions, an erratum notice of apology, or a withdrawal, which in some instances might be the remedy sought by the complainant.

publisher and author to some degree. If one looked only at formal legal relations, this would appear to be what is done. The reality, however, is notably different.

Contracts between authors and their publishers may theoretically be of infinite variety, but many conform to what is called the Minimum Terms Agreement (MTA). This has been drafted by the Society of Authors (along with the Writers' Guild, the nearest approximation to a trade union found in this highly individualistic craft), which has campaigned for inclusion of the provisions of the MTA in all agreements entered into between its members and any publisher. Though intended for use throughout the publishing industry, it is not quite a standard-form contract, in that individual firms may choose, and have chosen, to vary the wording slightly.[11]

Taking as an example the author's agreement used by Faber and Faber, two points may be highlighted. Much the most important is that the MTA requires the author to give warranties and indemnities satisfactory to the publisher to cover libel risks. This seems in part to be a formal way of concentrating the author's mind on the necessity of taking pains to avoid carelessness or venting personal spleen if either attitude would create possibilities of libel. 'Concentrate' rather than 'alert' seems the appropriate word, for the issue of libel does not arise for the first time when the publisher tenders a contract to the author. Rather, publishers depend upon authors alerting them to libel risks from the very beginning; in the words of one editor, 'that is absolutely integral to the process of preparing a book for publication and indeed commissioning it'. It is the job of the editor to, repeatedly, remind the author to look out for any potential problems. Writers of fiction not only must be concerned with unintentional defamation due to a coincidence of names,[12] but if, as is often the

---

[11] The MTA is not used throughout the entire industry; the larger firms are most likely to do so. It should be emphasized that libel is only a very small part of the MTA, which devotes many more paragraphs to copyright, and to royalties and other economic rights.   [12] See p. 132.

case, their work of fiction is based on real persons and events, they must take care that unflattering portraits do not come too close to being likenesses of identifiable individuals. Since it is not unknown for novelists to use fiction as a vehicle for lampooning their critics and former friends, this is a genuine problem for an editor, who has at best second-hand knowledge of whether the malignant buffoon depicted in the novel as a purported comic creation will soon materialize from the page with a solicitor's letter demanding a large sum of money.

For non-fiction, which produces complaints that are both far more frequent and carry the potential for much larger damages, the editor is dependent on assurances from the author that evidence purportedly documenting the misdeeds of some named person exists and is accessible. Since, as one case-hardened in-house solicitor put it, 'a lot of libel is not about truth, but about personal ego battle', blindly trusting the author's word would mean the editor was failing in his or her duty. In the end, however, publishers are dependent on their authors' trustworthiness and integrity, since they can hardly demand in every instance the sort of documentation a court would require in the relatively rare instances of litigation.

Every respondent reported that an indemnity was included in its contracts with authors, but nearly three-quarters reported that they would not enforce it. (Three commented that the situation was unsatisfactory.) Further, of the twelve who discussed the point, nine stated that they carried insurance for the author as well as for themselves. One obvious explanation of this apparent paradox is that most authors lack the funds necessary to cover major libel expenses. However, this is not the full story in the age of six-figure advances, especially since some claims may be relatively small. At least as important is the need to maintain amicable working relations with authors who may be expected to produce profits for the company in future. Short-term loss is bearable if there is a prospect of long-term gain. This attitude neatly replicates that found more than thirty years ago in a pioneering socio-legal study, which looked at relations between car dealers and manufacturers in the United States.[13] The reluctance to invoke the indemnity is not absolute; for example, one editor stated that if an author had acted 'maliciously', by which he meant deliberately making untruthful statements about someone, then in that 'most unusual' circumstance he would think hard about enforcement. Clearly, however, it is not a prospect that is likely to weigh heavily on many authors' shoulders, a view confirmed by Mark Le Fanu of the Society of Authors, who said that in practice liability would not arise 'so long as the author has acted honourably and has not been deceitful, or just stupid'. He did add, however, that many authors feel considerable anxiety about the inclusion of the clause in their contracts.

The second contractual matter is that where author and publisher agree that the book should be read for libel, the costs of that exercise are to be shared equally. This agreement had only come into effect in May 1993 so there was little experience to draw upon, and one informant with whom we raised this point could not say with certainty whether his firm, of which he was a director, would invoke this provision if an author refused to pay his share. He was clearly disinclined to treat it as a matter of automatically enforcing a legal obligation, yet also asked, 'What is the point of having it [the author's contribution requirement] there if you don't?' Since the cost of libel reading is relatively small,[14] this issue has not to our knowledge produced any notable conflict.

Conclusion: The Chilling Effect

'Every non-fiction publisher is in the libel business.' This assertion by one of our interviewees is amply borne out by the responses to the questionnaire. Even the two university presses reported libel problems resulting in heavy editing or withdrawal of some books. The effect of libel, however, is wider, deeper, and

---

[13] S. Macaulay, 'Non-contractual Relations in Business' (1963) 28 *Am.Soc.Rev* 45.   [14] See n. 4 above.

more insidious. In what seems to be a clear and increasing trend, publishers are seeking to avoid the risk of incurring expense by refraining from publishing material that might get them into trouble. Since 1994, one major conglomerate has received many fewer writs, because in that year it took a policy decision at board level, formalized in a policy statement issued to commissioning editors, to refuse to take on 'high risk' projects. 'High risk' meant primarily investigative works by journalists; certain subject matter, including anything to do with named police officers or sporting personalities; biography of living persons; and financial markets. In the following year another major company, which publishes magazines as well, was in process of deciding whether to 'pull the plug' on all investigative journalism. It had apparently been burned by the refusal of a source, which an author-journalist had insisted was reliable, to appear in court.

These changes in policy cannot be explained by an actual increase in the risk which publishers face, for no change in the law had occurred. What had changed, as one solicitor pointed out, was the *perception* of risk, as a result of steeply rising damages awards[15] and mounting fees charged by lawyers. The result is pervasive self-censorship for which no person or office is directly responsible, but which is just as powerful as direct prohibitions in stifling publication. The last word may best be left to an editor whose firm had undergone the experience of ten settlements in the five years:

The expense of the legal process is the key factor. We are to my bitter regret now self-censored by the horrendous costs. A robust defence of an obvious try-on without merit costs more than bunging some delinquent money to go away. Libel costs have become a major inhibition when it comes to publishing lively and thus possibly contentious non-fiction.

[15] It will be interesting, and important, to learn whether the diminution of awards that should result from the Court of Appeal decision in *John* v. *MGN Newspapers* [1996] 1 All ER 35, issued in Dec. 1995, will embolden publishers once again. It must be said, however, that the earlier decision in *Rantzen* v. *Mirror Group Newspapers* [1994] QB 670, which also suggested a less generous approach to damages, was the leading judgment during the period of our study and appears to have had little effect.

7

Magazines

Introduction

It is difficult to generalize about the impact of the libel regime on
the magazine industry as a whole, because the industry is so
heterogeneous in character. Magazines vary by size of circulation,
from radio and television listings magazines, each selling over
three million copies weekly, and consumer magazines like
Woman's Weekly, selling over one million, to special interest or
fringe political magazines selling a few thousand copies. They
vary also by frequency of publication: weekly, fortnightly,
monthly, quarterly, biannually, annually. Some are owned and
published by subsidiaries of multinational corporations and are
sold in significant quantities in other countries. Some are
extremely parochial, or struggle to survive financially from issue
to issue. With recent technical developments in desktop publishing and printing, the relatively much greater ease and lower cost
of producing a magazine in the first place have encouraged the
launching of new publications, including those for very small
potential markets. Accordingly, the birth and death rate of
magazines is much higher than is the case in other media.

In terms of numbers of published titles of all kinds, the
industry is made up of many hundreds of publishers responsible
for one or perhaps two magazines, spread all over the country.
However, in terms of total numbers of copies sold or in terms of
turnover, employment, and the other normal measures of size in
the media, the magazine industry is heavily concentrated in
London and the south-east. It is also dominated by half a dozen

major groups led by the International Publishing Corporation (IPC), now itself a subsidiary of the Anglo-Dutch conglomerate Reed Elsevier and linked with Reed Business Publications. IPC alone publishes over seventy different titles in over twenty different readership markets. Other major groups publishing a range of titles include Morgan-Grampian, Benn Brothers, East Midlands Allied Press, and Haymarket Press. Foreign publishing groups have made major incursions into British magazine publishing. The American presence is led by Condé Nast (with *Vogue*) and the National Magazine Company (with *Cosmopolitan* and *Good Housekeeping*). In addition to Elsevier, other European publishers, like the German group, Gruner & Jahr, have also broken into the British market. It will be readily apparent from the above outline of the industry that the incidence of libel-related activity, its editorial and commercial impact, and practices for handling it vary hugely from magazine to magazine across that wide spectrum.

Given the number and variety of magazine publishers in the United Kingdom, a comprehensive survey of the entire industry, even by way of questionnaire, was clearly not feasible. In any case we were fortunate that, at the time we were doing our research, the Periodical Publishers Association (PPA) was conducting a parallel libel enquiry among its members. The PPA is the umbrella trade association for the magazine-publishing industry in the United Kingdom. Although by no means all magazine publishers belong to the PPA, its membership of over 180 companies includes all the major magazine publishing-groups and, with the odd notable exception, most of the significant 'independent' magazine companies. The trigger for the PPA's initiative was the award by a libel jury in June 1993 of damages totalling £1,485,000 against the IPC magazine *Yachting World* for publishing a critical report on a new type of sailing trimaran. This award was the second highest ever made by a jury in a British libel case and sent a seismic shock through the magazine industry to which the PPA duly responded. It held an emergency meeting attended by some ninety editors and publishers in August 1994 and then sent out a libel questionnaire to all its members to be completed by the end of September 1994. We have been shown the PPA's summary of the responses to that questionnaire and we are grateful to the PPA for the substantial assistance this has been to our research. We did not seek to duplicate this with a questionnaire of our own. The PPA questionnaire asked respondents to identify the title or titles published by them in terms of the industry classifications in general usage: consumer magazines, business-to-business magazines, customer magazines, and 'other'.[1] It asked respondents to break down their titles by circulation and by approximate percentage of different kinds of subject matter (personalities; service features e.g. beauty, fashion; practical e.g. cookery, DIY; critical/review; news; product testing; listings; and 'other'). It then asked about the number of libel claims experienced, how they were disposed of, which category of editorial material provoked the claim, whether printers and distributors were joined in the claim in any way, how much the claims cost in damages and fees (either as a result of trial or out-of-court settlement), how many of the claims received were in their view justified, and how recent libel experience had changed the magazine's (or magazine group's) policies and practices, including decisions about libel insurance.

There were fifty-four responses to the questionnaire, twenty-one of them from publishers of consumer magazines, twenty-eight from publishers of business-to-business magazines, and five from publishers of customer magazines. The results of this survey

---

[1] In this classification, consumer magazines are those sold to the general consuming public, with the market dominated by publications devoted to women, life styles, television and other listings, leisure pursuits, etc.; business-to-business magazines, perhaps more widely known as trade magazines are published for those who work in a particular business, trade, or profession and are often distributed via subscription only or by free direct mail to a selected readership; and customer magazines are the small but rapidly growing market in magazines produced for a single client either for free distribution or sale to customers, for example the British Airways in-flight magazine for passengers or Sainsbury's magazine sold to customers at check-out desks.

will be discussed in the following section. It is the PPA's intention to conduct a similar survey during the summer of 1996 in order to monitor changes in libel experience in the three years since the *Yachting World* case. The 1996 survey will coincide roughly with the enactment of the 1996 Defamation Bill and thus provide a base line for subsequent investigations into the practical effect of the reforms contained in this new legislation.

In addition to the PPA survey we gathered evidence by way of structured interviews of the kind employed in our research on national newspapers. These were conducted with a range of group editors, editors of individual titles, publishers, and in-house lawyers employed by the major groups. In particular we interviewed those concerned with that small group of magazines which *prima facie* were likely to come into conflict with the law on defamation more regularly than the generality of magazines and which have featured over the years in a number of high-profile libel cases, namely the small number of weekly or fortnightly journals of opinion or satire, such as *The Economist*, the *Spectator*, the *New Statesman*, *Private Eye*, and *Scallywag*.

Statistical Information

In comparison with the other 'news' media covered by our research, the most obvious point to emerge is that the absolute number of libel actions, or 'serious' libel complaints settled out of court, is low.[2] Relative to the total number of titles and the total volume of copies sold by the industry as a whole in a year it is lower still. For the vast majority of magazines libel is not a regular part of the publishing process and looms as a potential rather than as an actual problem. For the handful of larger magazine publishing groups, however, and for the small group of opinion and satirical magazines mentioned above, libel business before and after publication has most of the same characteristics as those experienced by national and regional newspapers.

---

[2] Also see the low number of cases set down for trial: Ch. 2.

The results of the PPA survey were that of the twenty-one respondents from the publishers of consumer magazines nine had received a libel claim within the previous three years. These nine publishers between them had received seventy-seven individual complaints of alleged libel. Two of these seventy-seven complaints resulted in court action; forty-one were resolved through solicitors, involving some mixture of apology, damages, and costs; six were resolved without involving solicitors, but with some financial settlement; fourteen were resolved by way of printed apology; and fourteen were resolved 'at editor level'. Both the two cases which came to court were settled relatively cheaply: one at under £50,000 in total[3] and one at under £10,000. Of the claims settled out of court, two cost more than £15,000 and two cost more than £50,000. With business-to-business magazines the experience was similar. Of the twenty-eight respondents in this sector, sixteen had experienced a libel claim in the previous three years. These sixteen publishers between them had received ninety-three individual complaints of alleged libel. Two of these ninety-three cases resulted in court action; fifty-four were resolved through solicitors, involving some mixture of apology, damages, and costs; nineteen were resolved by way of printed apology; and eighteen were resolved 'at editor level'. The one court case that had been settled cost under £50,000. Of the claims settled out of court, six cost more than £15,000 and one cost more than £50,000. With the much smaller customer magazine group formal libel activity was even less significant. Of the five respondents, three had experienced a libel claim in the previous three years, but all three were settled 'at editor level' or, in one case, by a printed apology. None of the three cases involved more than £5,000.

Given this low level of libel activity and libel-related costs so far as typical magazine publishers are concerned, it is easy to see why the *Yachting World* case caused such commotion. However, the

---

[3] Figures for costs given in this section include legal costs and money paid by way of damages.

few opinion and satirical magazines, which are not typical in their content of the generality of magazines, have faced libel cases relatively more often and with much higher financial consequences. For example, in 1989 Mrs Sonia Sutcliffe, wife of the 'Yorkshire Ripper', was awarded a total of £600,000 in damages, including both compensatory and aggravated damages, against *Private Eye* for alleging that she had been paid £250,000 by the *Daily Mail* to write an account of her married life; and in 1993 the *New Statesman* paid out £250,000 by way of indemnities to meet the settlement costs of libel actions brought against its distributors and printers for an article referring to rumours of an affair between the Prime Minister, John Major, and Ms Clare Latimer, a freelance caterer working for No.10 Downing Street. (The £250,000 total was made up of about £90,000 paid in damages and the rest for costs.) In contrast to national newspapers and broadcasters, such cases for such magazines involve financial considerations that threaten to put them out of business.

Legal Procedures

In our own interviews we asked questions about the different arrangements that magazines or magazine groups made for handling libel. In general magazines do not have an in-house legal capacity. For most magazines a libel writ or a threat of one would be a new or rare experience. The majority of magazines are not checked for libel before publication and, if faced with a libel complaint, would deal with it on an *ad hoc* basis. Where a magazine belongs to a larger publishing group, for example the *Investors Chronicle* which is part of the Pearson Longman/ *Financial Times* group, it usually shares the same legal arrangements for libel advice as the other parts of the group. The small minority of magazines with regular exposure to substantial libel risk, for example the *New Statesman*, sometimes mirrored the arrangements on national newspapers by employing a lawyer, either a barrister or a solicitor, to read all or most of the copy for the coming issue on the day before the magazine went to press.

Such magazines then usually have a relationship with a particular firm of solicitors for dealing with libel matters arising after publication. If the magazine is one of those with libel insurance, this firm of solicitors will normally also act for the insurers. Indeed in most cases insurers require as part of the insurance policy that the magazine be advised by an 'approved' firm of solicitors with known libel experience.

In the case of the two or three major magazine publishing groups, in-house legal expertise exists in much the same way as it does for a national newspaper. In these few cases the publishing company will employ a lawyer or lawyers to look after all its legal interests. This work will be commercial as well as editorial and the amount of the in-house lawyer's time devoted to libel will vary. In recent years, particularly since the *Yachting World* case, awareness of libel risks and risk management have been much greater in the main magazine publishing groups. Given the range and volume of material published within a major group in any week, comprehensive pre-publication scrutiny of all material is usually not possible, and no system equivalent to national newspapers' 'night-lawyer' arrangements is employed. However, editors and their staffs are made aware of the need to refer potentially contentious material to the in-house lawyer for discussion and clearance. In practice, therefore, the in-house lawyer in these groups exercises the same kind of powerful influence that national newspaper in-house lawyers have on the redrafting of wording and the striking out of all or parts of articles where it would be difficult to mount an effective legal defence in the event of a writ being received. Modern production methods and communication systems, with networked computers and fax machines, makes it easy in a way that would not have been the case five years ago for a magazine-group lawyer based with the company's headquarters management to be consulted before publication and, indeed, to call up draft articles on screen for detailed consideration.

As an indication of the greater attention and resources devoted to libel in the magazine industry since 1993, IPC now employs a second in-house lawyer whose time is almost wholly devoted to libel, though covering both IPC magazines and Reed Business Press publications. Personal arrangements and historical accident also play a part in libel arrangements, even within large groups. For example, a particular title, even a major one within a large group, may make its own 'freelance' arrangement for pre-publication legal advice. Some magazines with bad past libel experiences prefer not to rely just on 'alarm bells ringing' in the minds of editors or sub-editors and to bear the cost of having all pages read by a lawyer, but these are very much a minority. Arrangements within the large groups for dealing with libel issues arising after publication tend to be governed by the current workload of the in-house lawyer or lawyers. They may handle negotiations themselves; or, if they are at that moment overloaded or if the case threatens to be complicated, they may put the work out, usually to one of a small number of solicitors with whom they have regular contact.

Factors Specific to Magazines

In general the factors taken into account with regard to libel, both before publication and in respect of tactical decisions on how to handle complaints arising out of publication, are the same for magazines as for other print media. These factors, therefore, will not be rehearsed again here. The kind of subject matter giving rise to libel complaints is similar. Replies to the PPA survey cited articles and features about 'personalities' and 'news' items as the areas giving rise to most problems. It seemed, as might be expected, that business-to-business magazines produced more libel problems than consumer magazines, since adverse comment in a magazine widely read in a particular business or trade has the potential to do serious commercial damage to a company or firm. On the basis of anecdotal evidence about business-to-business magazines, out-of-court settlements in the £25,000 range, while not numerous, were not regarded as exceptional either. In contrast, as a result of complaints arising from its consumer magazines, a large magazine group might only expect in any one year to make a small number of settlements at or below £5,000. With trade magazines, most complaints would typically be expected in relation to stories involving sub-contractors failing to make payments, or the activities of directors of haulage companies, or shady business practices of one kind or another. With consumer magazines, particular libel problems stressed by our interviewees included the private lives of pop stars, particularly if any claim or innuendo of drug-taking was involved, or coverage of their business interests; cases involving doctors and nurses brought by the Medical Defence Union; restaurant reviews; certain named individuals with a reputation for being litigious; and classes of persons represented by agents of one kind or another, who see it as their function to trawl for possible libel actions. The detail naturally varies from title to title, but in general in these respects there is nothing exceptional about the nature of the libel experience of magazines.

There are, however, a number of ways in which libel impacts specifically and differently on magazines, and these will now be explored in relation to the evidence we collected. We consider here first the large number of magazines which serve a specialized readership or a particular business. The small group of magazines whose editorial *raison d'être* is to comment on public affairs and to challenge or mock authority raises important issues of public policy in respect of libel, but these will be commented upon separately.

The key distinction between magazines in general and, say, national newspapers is that magazines have no commercial motivation to press at the boundaries of defamation in what they publish. This is because their circulation, readership, and profitability do not in general depend on competing with other publications by way of disclosure or sensationalism. So far as business-to-business magazines are concerned, many of them are in any case not sold on newsstands but are distributed by 'controlled circulation' to selected target readerships. Even consumer magazines, which are sold to the general public on newsstands, sell themselves mainly on the visual image projected by the front cover and the regular quality of their editorial 'mix'. They do not rely, as popular newspapers do, on striking front-page stories and eye-catching headlines, which tend to be areas of journalism giving rise to high libel risk. The magazine industry's whole approach to libel is conditioned by this important commercial reality, which militates strongly against taking libel risks.

In some specific cases the reputation of a magazine in its market niche may well depend quite heavily on its record in reporting facts and investigating issues, relating for example to a specific industry, that have not been covered elsewhere in the general media. In other cases, as with *Yachting World*, the magazine may consider that for strategic commercial reasons it has no option but to take the risk and bear the cost of going to court in order to defend the credibility and editorial integrity of the publication. But as a generalization for magazines, unlike national newspapers, running deliberate libel risks for good editorial and commercial reasons is very unusual. Whereas the national media tend to regard libel and its associated costs as a normal and relatively high operating expense that has to be borne as an unavoidable part of being in the business, this attitude is absolutely not part of the culture of the overwhelming majority of magazines. With rare exceptions magazine managements and their legal advisers do not see it as their role or duty to bear the risks and costs of fighting 'test cases' in order to establish principles. The practical consequence of this culture, we were told, is that the attitude 'if in doubt, strike it out' is strongly entrenched in most magazines.

The second major difference with magazines is that in most of their organizational structures there is a 'publisher' or 'general manager' alongside the editor, who is responsible for all the commercial aspects of the magazine. The publisher normally has a higher managerial status within the company than the editor. This structural characteristic of magazines in most cases has the effect of tilting the balance of consideration both before and after publication in the direction of taking the commercially least risky line and against any idea of standing up for some abstract concept of editorial autonomy. The combined effect of both these two distinctive characteristics of the magazine industry is that in most cases there is no strong commercial or editorial incentive to publish wording that will attract readers' attention, but will run measurable libel risk. Indeed there is every incentive to argue that, taking an issue of a magazine as a whole, it cannot be worth running for no commercial gain a single article, or a sentence in an article, that might end up costing the magazine £20,000.

Journals of Opinion

So far in this Chapter we have been concerned with the impact of libel on the great mass of magazines of various kinds published in the United Kingdom. In general it can be said that they try to avoid becoming entangled in the libel process, and that for the most part they succeed. We shall now consider the small group of regularly-published magazines which court controversy, challenge reputations, and express opinions. As a consequence their libel risk is high. Often, also, such magazines lack the large financial backing available to the national media. For this group, libel is an ever-present concern.

Among this group the fortnightly satirical magazine *Private Eye* stands out for its attitude towards and experience of libel. Now in its fourth decade of publication, the magazine has become the mature grandfather of 'alternative' magazines. As one observer recently put it: 'Though it still looks like it's laid out by badly hung-over undergraduates, it has become an institution, the gadfly buzzing the heads of state'.[4] Every issue that it publishes is replete with deliberately defamatory material, since its overt purpose is to rubbish reputations and to expose hypocrisy. In very exceptional circumstances a draft article may be submitted to a lawyer for comment before publication, but in

---

[4] Morning Edition, National Public Radio, 15 Oct. 1991.

general decisions on whether or what to publish are taken by the editor alone. The magazine's attitude towards 'fact checking' has always been somewhat cavalier. Whereas the mainstream media strive not to publish or broadcast material which could not be defended in court with the evidence of credible witnesses, *Private Eye* has always operated on the principle that its function is to publish allegations which its 'nose' tells it to be true, even when legally admissible evidence is lacking. In carrying out this function, the magazine has in roughly equal measure earned a positive reputation for exposing matters of public interest where other media are inhibited from doing so by the libel regime and a negative reputation for professional shoddiness for its practice of printing rumour and gossip as if they were fact. Unlike other media outlets it has not hesitated to publish risky material about individuals known for their propensity to sue, for example the publisher, Mr Robert Maxwell, the entrepreneur, Sir James Goldsmith, or the cricketer, Mr Ian Botham. The magazine's attitude towards libel complaints received as a result of publication is also untypical of other branches of the media. It often publishes letters before action from solicitors, or comments in print on complaints received in a way that, from the point of view of conventional libel tactics, could only be regarded as reckless.

In short, *Private Eye* behaves editorially in a way that seems to ignore or defy what most branches of the media see as the restrictive nature of the British libel regime. The fact that it has survived and indeed prospered over more than thirty-five years would seem to indicate that the regime cannot be too inhibiting, even for muckraking publications. Its circulation is now in excess of 200,000 per issue. In part this insouciant attitude has been the result of a deliberate editorial and commercial decision that there was both a serious journalistic purpose and money to be made in publishing articles that the conventional media regarded as 'too hot to handle'. In part it has been based on a calculated view that most of its targets are unlikely to wish in the end to expose themselves as plaintiffs in court. The magazine's attitude to libel in making its publishing decisions may in large measure have contributed to its reputation and helped what started out as an 'alternative' publication in the 1960s to become something of a media institution, but it has also meant that the magazine has lived dangerously over a financial chasm that from time to time has threatened to engulf it in legal costs.

In 1976–7, for example, *Private Eye* became embroiled in a series of libel actions, including one of criminal libel, brought by Sir James Goldsmith, which involved thirteen court hearings before the matter was finally settled out of court for a payment of £30,000. A decade later, an unsubstantiated allegation that Mr Robert Maxwell was bankrolling the then Labour Leader of the Opposition, Neil Kinnock, in the hope of an eventual peerage, made as part of a deliberate campaign of vilification sustained over a prolonged period, cost the magazine over £300,000 in damages. The £600,000 libel damages awarded by a jury against *Private Eye* to Mrs Sonia Sutcliffe in 1989 have already been cited. In terms of libel, it may be said that the case of *Private Eye* is *sui generis*. Other alternative magazines, for example *Scallywag*, with much smaller circulations and resources, rely for protection on the fact that potential plaintiffs will refrain from suing in order to avoid giving wider publicity to allegations and because the likelihood in practice of being able to collect substantial damages or costs from them is low.

If *Private Eye* is untypical of other journals of opinion in respect of its attitude to libel, this group of magazines still shares other problems with the libel system as it currently operates.

First, the quantum of damages and the level of costs involved in libel cases are out of proportion to the budgets of most such magazines. Even a magazine with the underlying profitability of *Private Eye* today cannot absorb £600,000 damages awards, plus the much higher associated costs, and remain solvent. It has from time to time been forced to resort to special appeals to its readership to enable it to continue in existence. Other magazines, even those with a far more cautious attitude towards libel, are less fortunately placed. A *cause célèbre* involved an action against the right-wing *Spectator* in 1957 brought by the Labour politicians

Aneurin Bevan and Richard Crossman and the Labour Party general secretary, Morgan Phillips, and funded by the socialist millionaire, Howard Samuel, over an article which implied (probably rightly) that the three of them were drunk much of the time during an international socialist congress in Venice. The plaintiffs were awarded £2,500 each, plus costs, a total sum in 1957 which posed a serious financial threat to the magazine's survival. During the period of our own researches, the actions brought in 1993 by John Major and Ms Latimer against the left-wing *New Statesman* and its printers and distributors cost the magazine a total of over £250,000. This was a significant factor in destroying its existing financial structure and forcing it to seek new ownership and recapitalization. In the face of such sums magazines with limited financial resources can only offer what has come to be termed the 'Armageddon' or 'Doomsday' defence, namely the counter-threat that the publisher will be forced into liquidation and that then any damages and costs awarded will consequently be irrecoverable.

Secondly, small-circulation magazines are particularly vulnerable to printers and distributors being joined as defendants in libel proceedings. This is for a number of reasons. The printers and distributors have no commercial interest in mounting a defence against a libel writ and every commercial incentive to settle at once. Where under the terms of their contractual arrangements with the magazine publisher they are free to conduct their own libel proceedings, the fact that a printer or distributor has settled quickly with a plaintiff undermines any subsequent defence that the publisher may wish to mount. Where the contractual arrangements require the publisher to indemnify the printer and distributor there is in addition no pressure operating on them to seek to limit damages or costs. Since the magazines in this category are by their nature of relatively small circulation, the value of the continuing business does not provide the incentive for the printer or distributor to hold the line and support the publisher that might exist in the case of a large circulation publication.

Thirdly, small-circulation magazines which depend on news-stand sales to the general public are correspondingly threatened if, for commercial reasons linked to libel, distributors are persuaded not to handle them. The newspaper and magazine wholesale and retail business in the United Kingdom is effectively monopolized by two companies, W. H. Smith and John Menzies. If either or both of these companies decline to handle a magazine that relies heavily on its newsstand sale, it becomes *ipso facto* unviable.

The John Major/*New Statesman* case in 1993 raised several issues of public concern in these respects. Libel writs are normally served on authors, editors, and publishers. Previously it had been rare for *bona fide* litigants to join printers and distributors in libel actions, though some, like Sir James Goldsmith and Robert Maxwell, had used the tactic not so much in search of damages but as a way of preventing dissemination. In this case, the *New Statesman*'s printers, BPCC, settled rapidly with the two litigants for a total of some £25,000, submitted costs of more than double that amount, and subsequently cancelled the printing contract. The distributors, Comag, settled with both plaintiffs at a somewhat lower total level of damages and costs. W. H. Smith, even though it was engaged at the same time in the campaign to prevent the government levying VAT on newspapers and magazines, settled for the least amount of all three, mindful no doubt of the dangerous precedent that was being set for distributors. The substantive case against the magazine never came to trial. The *New Statesman* at an early stage paid £1,001 into court. Having settled separately with BPCC, Comag, and W. H. Smith, the plaintiffs took the £1,001 and claimed their taxed costs. The total direct bill to the magazine was about £70,000. The total payments made under indemnities covering printers and distributors were almost three times as high.

In this *New Statesman* case the terms of the contractual indemnities with the printers and distributors gave the magazine no control over the conduct of their defences but required it to meet the costs of their settlements in full. This arrangement, which seemed to be widespread in the industry, is clearly unsatisfactory for the magazine publisher. Other magazine publishers, particularly the larger ones, offer indemnities to their printers and publishers, but stipulate that the conduct of defences should be in their own hands, so that the terms of the indemnity do not cover printers and distributors who wish for whatever reason to mount their own defences and reach their own settlements. In the light of the *New Statesman* case, one would expect this latter kind of indemnity to become more normal. The extension of the defence of innocent dissemination contained in the 1996 Defamation Act may slow a trend towards more widespread joining of printers and distributors in libel actions, though it remains to be seen how the new provisions work out in practice.

Finally, a fourth respect in which the libel regime specially affects this group of journals of opinion derives from the fact that they mostly have very small permanent staffs and rely heavily on freelance contributors over whom they have far less control. This means that in reaching editorial judgements about the libel risk involved in publishing more has to be taken on trust. Much more inhibiting, however, is the fact that, when a libel complaint or writ is received, the mounting of a defence cannot rely on the availability and commitment that could be expected if it depended on information and evidence supplied by a full-time member of staff. In the first place a freelance contributor is normally only paid for publication rights to what has been written and not to assist in legal proceedings. In the second place, the freelance journalist responsible for the article being complained of may literally not be available for further consultation. In these circumstances a magazine's capacity to defend a libel action is clearly circumscribed.

Insurance Arrangements

At the time that we were beginning our researches there appeared to be a general impression that insurance arrangements for the magazine industry were unsatisfactory. The number of firms offering libel insurance was contracting. Two of the major Lloyd's syndicates previously involved had just ceased writing new business. At the same time the level of premiums being demanded was rising sharply, as was the level of the 'excess' being included in the terms of insurance policies, i.e., the level below which in each case the costs are to be born directly by the magazine publisher. A common observation at the time was that magazines were paying more and more and getting less and less cover. A number of magazines around this time decided to drop their insurance policies and to adopt total 'self-insurance'. Some small magazine publishers also expressed to us the view that they disliked the conflict of interest involved in the fact that insurers normally also instructed the magazine's own solicitors to act for them as well. In practice the result, they thought, was that when the cost of a particular case reached the level of the excess set in the insurance policy the solicitors involved switched from primarily acting for the magazine to primarily acting for the insurers. Clearly the insurers' interests centre purely on commercial considerations and on settling the case as cheaply as possible. This interest may well conflict with the editorial and indeed commercial concerns of the magazine. This feeling also led some magazines at the time to drop all libel insurance.

The boards of other magazine companies, however, including those of the major groups, preferred to maintain the comfort of an insurance safety net against disaster. Our impression is that at the time we were concluding our research and subsequently the trend against libel insurance has been reversed. Factors encouraging this reverse have probably been the number of large libel settlements that attracted substantial press coverage in the mid-1990s, including specifically the *Yachting World* case itself; and the entrance into the market of new insurers prepared to write libel business.

Conclusions

While libel does not play such a prominent part in the editorial and managerial life of the mainstream magazines as it does for national newspapers, the tendency from the mid-1990s has been for there to be a greatly heightened awareness of libel issues in the industry. This is evidenced by the fact that, in the aftermath of the *Yachting World* case, the Periodical Publishers Association published, in conjunction with the British Society of Magazine Editors and the British Association of Industrial Editors, guidelines written by its legal consultant, Peter Mason, on the avoidance and handling of libel claims. In the event the *Yachting World* case was not followed by the widely expected flood of copycat libel actions that might have caused insurmountable problems for that part of the magazine industry concerned with product testing and reviewing. However, the industry as a whole evidently adjusted its practices to the evidence that magazines were receiving a greater number of libel-related complaints than in the past. Libel-awareness training has become much more routine for journalists in the magazine industry and the PPA reports an increasing level of enquiries from its members about libel insurance. It will be interesting to see what light the PPA's 1996 survey of its members libel experience throws on these trends.

8

The Scottish Media

Introduction

The research methodology adopted in relation to the media in Scotland was a little different from that used in England for a number of reasons. First, the population served by the Scottish media is significantly smaller, which itself means that the number of claims for defamation made will also be significantly smaller: the statistical information gathered was, therefore, too limited to draw from it any useful general conclusions. Secondly, again as a result of the small size of the jurisdiction, it was considered appropriate to look at a broad cross-section of the media rather than to separate out the different forms, as has been done in the English chapters. Thirdly, much of the media output disseminated in Scotland comes from England, where the individual organization's policies are set and where the legal risks are assessed (not always accurately, as shown in the related field of election law when in May 1995 the Court of Session interdicted the BBC from broadcasting within Scotland three days before the Scottish local elections a *Panorama* interview with the Prime Minister). For this reason it was decided to concentrate on media outlets primarily based in Scotland. And fourthly, the management of defamation risk by Scottish media organizations follows a different pattern from that in England, with only one of those organizations investigated, BBC Scotland, employing an in-house lawyer. All others contract out their media law work to private firms of solicitors (though interestingly many of the larger organizations, such as Scottish Television and Caledonian Newspapers Ltd, employ in-house solicitors for non-media law work such as contract, conveyancing, employment, and the like). Much of the work for the present project, therefore, had to be directed towards firms of solicitors. However, this did bring with it a significant advantage, in that most of the firms contacted had a number of media clients in addition to the media company we were concerned with in this project. So while series of interviews were conducted with a relatively small number of individual solicitors, the range of media organizations they represent is very wide and includes many English publishers and broadcasters who disseminate material in Scotland. In addition, most of these solicitors undertake pursuer work as well as defender work, and are able to see, and comment upon, the operation of the law of defamation in Scotland from both sides.

The methodology adopted in this part of the study was to interview personally the editors of two Glasgow-based newspapers (the *Herald*, a national daily, and the *Evening Times*, a local evening paper), the chief executive of one newspaper group (Caledonian Newspapers), and then to conduct fortnightly telephone interviews (after an initial face-to-face meeting) with the solicitors employed by these two newspapers and by BBC Scotland. These interviews covered three separate (but over-lapping) periods of between two to three months in 1994. One-off interviews were also conducted with solicitors employed by Scottish Television and by the Edinburgh-based Scotsman Publications Ltd, primarily for the purpose of confirming the information received during the series of interviews, and as a check against relying too heavily on what might have proved to be an unrepresentative or maverick individual. In addition, one interview was conducted with the owner and managing director of a small independent production company, which produces radio programmes, primarily but not exclusively broadcast by BBC Scotland.

As with sections of the English media, as described in other chapters, questionnaires were circulated to all the solicitors involved, though the rate of return was minimal and no useful hard statistical information was acquired by this means. However, some interesting comments were made on such questionnaires as were returned, which served to back up things that had been said in the interviews. The conclusions drawn in this Chapter are arrived at by and large from the interviews themselves, and the general approach is therefore more one of examining attitudes than of analysing statistics.

One of the major focuses of this Chapter is to explore some of the reasons, or perceived reasons, why the level of defamation claims before the Scottish courts is so much less than in England, and to see whether this prevents the 'chilling effect' of defamation being felt, or causes it to be felt significantly less, in Scotland. Judging purely from the law reports, the number of defamation cases to reach the Scottish courts is far lower than can be explained by the smaller population alone, and the suspicion that the number of potential pursuers who seek legal advice on potential claims for defamation is similarly much smaller in Scotland was borne out by the experiences of the solicitors questioned.

In order to put the Scottish position in perspective for the general reader (who may be assumed to be more familiar with the position in England) it is proposed to describe, briefly, some of the major differences in both law and practice between the two jurisdictions. Much of the questioning of Scottish practitioners (which will be described later in this Chapter) was designed to identify which, if any, of these differences explained the relative paucity of cases before the Scottish courts.

Legal differences between Scotland and England

As well as the practical and procedural differences described below, there are a number of (fairly minor, it has to be admitted) differences in substantive law between the two jurisdictions, some of which may play a role in discouraging claims in Scotland.

Defamation in Scotland is a purely civil wrong, unlike in England where in some circumstances libel can be a crime. This might encourage the Scots to see defamation as a less significant harm and one, therefore, less worth pursuing. There is no technical difference between the written libel and the spoken slander, and the proper terminology for both is 'defamation', though the words libel and slander are sometimes used.

The classes of privileged communications are slightly different between the two jurisdictions. In England parties to a civil action are entitled to absolute privilege for statements made in the course of the legal proceedings, while in Scotland they are entitled to qualified privilege only. Similarly, reports of judicial proceedings in England are protected by absolute privilege, while the Scottish courts, after some apparent hestitation, settled upon granting merely qualified privilege to such reports.[1] These rules in theory make it slightly easier for pursuers to sue in Scotland than in England, but, in practice, in most cases proving even qualified privilege will provide a sufficient defence to the defender. These differences are, therefore, of minimal significance.

Two features of Scots law, already mentioned in Chapter 1, suggest that pursuers in Scotland have a more difficult time than plaintiffs in England. First, the defence of fair comment seems to be rather wider in Scotland than in England, for there is not the emphasis on the honesty of the comment that exists in England, and the defence can be validly stated in Scotland so long as the comment is relevant to the facts being commented upon. Secondly, legal aid is not only unavailable for defamation, but is not available either for verbal injury (the Scottish equivalent of malicious falsehood), so it is not open to a pursuer to raise a legally aided action by pleading verbal injury rather than defamation (as can happen in England). On the other hand, the rule in Scotland is that the claim for damages is not destroyed by

---

[1] However, the Defamation Act 1996 extends the absolute privilege for fair and accurate contemporaneous reports of legal proceedings to Scotland, as well as England (where there had probably been such a privilege under the Libel Amendment Act 1888).

the death of either the pursuer or the defender (as is the case in England). Moreover, a Scottish executor can continue an action brought by a pursuer before death and can obtain both damages for patrimonial loss and solatium for (the deceased's) hurt feelings; and can raise an action after the pursuer's death in order to recover patrimonial loss to the deceased's estate.

All these differences are fairly minor, and they seem to balance each other out to a large extent. It can be concluded, therefore, that the differences in legal rules will have little practical effect on the level of defamation claims. Far more significant are the practical and procedural differences which exist between the two jurisdictions.

Practical and procedural differences between Scotland and England

As mentioned in the introduction to this Chapter, one noticeable difference in defamation practice between Scotland and England is the fact that only one organization, BBC Scotland, employs an in-house lawyer to deal with its media law work. All the others contract the work out. This may seem surprising in the light of another noticeable difference: the almost complete absence of a specialist defamation bar, or even specialist media law firms. It is true that a small number of firms in Scotland deal with a sizeable percentage of the defamation work that is available (particularly defender work), but none of the solicitors interviewed saw him- or herself as belonging to a specialist media law firm and it would be fair to say that no firm in Scotland could survive on defamation work alone, or even more generally media law work alone. All the firms interviewed are (in Scottish terms at least) sizeable partnerships which undertake a large variety of commercial and domestic legal work.

The major practical difference between Scotland and England, and the one which, at the end of the day, may be the most straightforward and most readily understandable explanation for the lower number of claims, is the fact that in Scotland the level of damages which will be awarded to a successful pursuer in an action for defamation is significantly lower than the level of damages awarded by English courts. Scots law does not accept the notion of punitive or exemplary damages in the field of defamation or any other claim, and the assessment of damages follows as closely as possible the assessment of loss that the pursuer can establish. This is not to say that only patrimonial or economic loss can be claimed: a pursuer can seek what is called 'solatium', that is to say an amount of damages which will act as a solace to his or her hurt feelings or the affront that he or she has suffered. Economic loss, if proved, can be substantial. The largest award traced was made in 1979 to an insurance company which was able to prove that a newspaper article alleging that the pursuer ran a 'disreputable' business had caused it to lose a substantial amount of business: damages assessed at £327,000 (before interest and expenses) were awarded. One organization interviewed is at the time of writing being sued for £750,000, most of which is made up of lost earnings allegedly suffered by an advocate (barrister) whose professional integrity was allegedly challenged in a newspaper article. However, traditionally awards of solatium have been modest and the court is likely to assess what is needed as a solace in hundreds rather than in thousands of pounds. One judge in 1982 felt able to describe a claim for £10,000 (made by a policeman who alleged hurt feelings when a person he arrested complained to the chief constable) as 'ridiculous', and awarded £200. On the other hand, there is some evidence from the law reports that the value of awards of solatium is increasing. In 1991 a sum of £50,000 was awarded (by a jury) to a female prison warder who was accused in a newspaper of having had a sexual relationship with a prisoner. (That figure, however, was justified by much more severe emotional distress than mere affront to dignity, and the claim bordered indeed on a case of psychiatric illness). In the same year an allegation that the pursuer was a war criminal was indicated by the trial judge (sitting without a jury) to be likely to attract around £35,000, which is very much less than the £1,500,000 that an English jury awarded Lord Aldington for a very similar allegation in 1990.

Another important procedural difference is that jury trials for defamation are almost unknown in Scotland. Juries remain competent, and indeed under the relevant legislation[2] defamation actions are amongst the 'enumerated causes' for jury trial rather than a hearing before a judge alone (known as a 'proof'). However, the parties can agree to a proof rather than a trial, or, if there is no agreement, the court can order a proof rather than a trial on being shown by one or other of the parties that there is 'special cause' for doing so. There have been a few cases in which 'special cause' has been discussed and defined by the court and the test is fairly strict. It is perhaps surprising, therefore, that jury trials are so rare (only two have been traced since the Second World War). One interviewee who raised this matter (and who does pursuer work as well as defender work) speculated that pursuers in Scotland recognize the unpredictability of juries, and do not perceive them as having a bias in favour of the pursuer. One can speculate further on the character of the Scots, which might include a tendency to trust a judge rather than a panel of laymen, as well as a lack of sympathy towards someone complaining about affront and hurt feelings. These are matters that can be tested only by future study directed towards the motivation of pursuers. The fact remains that there is no great pressure by pursuers in Scotland to insist on jury trials, and the vast majority of cases that do get to court are conducted before a judge alone.

An important procedural difference between Scotland and England, though one which would be felt only when actions are raised, concerns methods of pleading. A Scottish pursuer must show at a preliminary stage that the words or communications complained of are capable of defaming him or her, and if this cannot be done the case is dismissed as irrelevant before the trial or proof. The English plaintiff may (in theory) get to court before

---

[2] Court of Session Act 1988, s. 11.

that question is answered,[3] with the result that potentially non-defamatory statements can be put before a jury. The practical effect is that once an action is raised it is easier to 'kill it off' in Scotland than in England.

The Operation of Defamation Law in Scotland

In order to obtain information about how the law of defamation operates in Scotland and its practical effect, a number of interviews was conducted, as described in the Introduction above. Three series of interviews were carried out, two with solicitors representing particular newspapers, and one with the in-house solicitor for BBC Scotland. The interviews with a national[4] daily newspaper were carried out on a fortnightly basis between 22 April 1994 and 1 July 1994; with a local evening newspaper between 15 April 1994 and 4 July 1994; and with BBC Scotland between 11 August 1994 and 1 November 1994. In addition, single interviews were held in early 1995 with the solicitor representing Scottish Television (and Channel 4 in Scotland, Borders Television, ITN in Scotland, and the Scottish editions of the *Daily Sport* and the *Sunday Sport*), and with the solicitor representing The Scotsman Publications Ltd (and various local radio stations).

Time spent on defamation work

The first set of questions that was addressed to the interviewees was aimed at quantifying the amount of their professional time that was spent on defamation work. They were requested to limit their answers to the single publication or broadcaster that they

---

[3] However, under an amendment to RSC, Ord. 82 introduced in 1994, either party may apply to a judge in chambers to determine the meaning of the words and whether as pleaded they are defamatory, so the difference in the text may be now of more theoretical than practical importance.

[4] 'National' in Scottish terms.

were being primarily interviewed for. The solicitor for the national daily considered that she spent between a quarter and a third of her time on defamation work for that particular client, which was roughly the same for the other newspaper representative, though (very unusually) he spends almost 100 per cent of his total professional time on defamation work. The answers given to questions over the interview period tended to suggest that these estimates were fairly typical. In relation to the national daily, the solicitor reported that her time was spent dealing both with post-publication complaints and with prepublication checking. At the initial interview she was dealing with three post-publication complaints.[5] The following fortnight proved fairly quiet with about twenty hours being spent by members of the firm on defamation work for that newspaper. The next period was similarly quiet, and the solicitor spent most of her time doing library-based research, as part of preparation for a major case; and in order to defend another case on the basis of the pursuer's bad character some research was necessary to discover how far Scots law allows averments of general reputation. The following two periods of a fortnight each were also quiet, though work was again starting to pick up towards the beginning of July.

The second series of interviews was conducted with the solicitor for a local evening paper. At the initial interview, he reported receiving on average ten enquiries a day either from journalists direct or from the editor in relation to stories not yet published and in relation to complaints that had been received. Most of his time, however, is spent reviewing unsubbed stories concerning which the journalist or editor has some worry about its potential defamatory content. The following two-week period was reported to be particularly busy, due to two big serializations which had already started on contentious issues, and the imminent commencement of a serialization of a boardroom battle at one of the Glasgow football clubs. The following period had

[5] That did not include the major case which was then pending against the organization in which an advocate was suing for £750,000.

been dominated by news of John Smith's (the Leader of the Opposition's) death and the conviction of Scottish child-murderer Robert Black, neither of which stories was likely to cause legal problems, and they tended to squeeze out more problematical items, resulting in a much quieter time than normal for this solicitor. The following period was reported to be average and the last two-week period again quieter (early July 1994).

As already noted, the BBC is the only organization that employs an in-house solicitor, and not surprisingly he reported spending a larger percentage of this time on defamation work for that single organization than the other two. He reported spending on average about half his time on defamation matters, with the other half being taken up with other media law issues, in particular contempt. The first two periods of a fortnight were particularly busy in relation to defamation owing to the receipt of a writ from a football club for £2 million, and to the preparation work in relation to a case raised some time previously by a housing association, for which a date had just been set for the proof.[6] The following fortnight was again reported to be busy, for two reasons: the calling of a case in court (though the case was quickly adjourned) and because the new political and Parliamentary season was about to commence, involving the checking of a number of potentially controversial issues. The final period was reported to be about average.

Conclusions on Time Spent

The amount of time spent on defamation work varied tremendously between the three solicitors interviewed. This seemed to be related to the nature of the newspaper or broadcaster that they represented. So the highest profile organization, the BBC, requires more actual time to be spent, because of the greater likelihood that it will attract complaints (and also, perhaps, because the level of damages might be increased due to the wide

---

[6] This case was subsequently settled on the day the action was due to call.

dissemination of material broadcast nationally). For the national daily newspaper, material is checked carefully pre-publication, but it is less likely to run 'racy' stories, such as serializations of boardroom battles in football clubs, with the result that the amount of legal work necessary is rather less. The local evening newspaper, though it has a smaller catchment area, is more inclined to take risks with what it wants to say, and is more inclined, therefore, to seek quick legal advice, burdening this paper's legal adviser rather more than the legal advisers of the national daily. These conclusions are reflected in the work of the solicitor who acts for various publications from The Scotsman Publications Ltd. The quality Sunday newspaper they publish, *Scotland on Sunday*, is investigative and high risk and creates a significant amount of legal work. The quality daily, *The Scotsman*, was described as 'fairly safe' and it seldom gets into difficulties. One of their evening newspapers, being more sensational but less investigative, lies somewhere in between.

Major rewriting

The next set of questions was designed to identify how often the publisher or broadcaster was advised to rewrite or redraft a particular story or feature. No interviewee reported having to advise that a story be completely scrapped, at least not for reason of fears of liability for defamation. All three reported regularly suggesting small changes and, sometimes, changes of emphasis. The following comment in relation to prepublication screening, by the solicitor for the national daily, was typical:

There is always a comment that can be made about some aspect of a story. It's usually to the effect that some small thing should be changed, words here and there. We don't read the paper from cover to cover. What we read are things that are given to us which other people think are risky in some way and so it's not surprising that we make comments on nearly everything and suggest small changes on everything. But we very seldom recommend a complete rewrite or that a story should be scrapped. Last month we did say 'Scrap this completely', but that is rare. It was because the journalist had given far too much detail about a trial that was going on. In other words, he had gone beyond the boundaries of the Contempt Act and that's more serious since it is criminal.

In each of the following interviews over the whole period, this solicitor reported that she had never suggested a major rewrite of a story.

The solicitor for the evening local paper gave a slightly different response. To the question, 'How often do you advise a major rewriting of a story or feature to avoid libel risks?', he replied as follows:

Never. I tell them to take out words, to change things here and there. There is never a major rewriting. I tell them that you just cannot run a story when there is only one individual's word for it. For example just yesterday the paper wanted to run a story about a woman who went to the hairdresser and had her head burned by some chemicals in the shampoo. But the reporter had only spoken to the woman. I told them that they had to speak to the doctor, the health visitor and the hairdresser. That wasn't a story, because it hadn't been written properly.

In later interviews this solicitor reported never recommending any change that meant an alteration to the thrust of a story or the way it was written, or removing any factual allegation.

The BBC solicitor, again, gave a different account. On two occasions during the period investigated he recommended changes which, in his view, were major. The first concerned the final programme in the series *Billy Connolly's World Tour of Scotland*. Much of this programme was a monologue by Billy Connolly and in one recording he had made a number of fairly rude jokes about (named) famous explorers who had got lost. The solicitor had at the back of his mind that one of them had previously sued in England in respect of some joke that had been told against him, and after some research had discovered that he had obtained £100,000. The whole of the programme had to be 'rejigged' to ensure the troublesome material was removed. Interestingly, it was reported that the potential defamation was not particularly bad, but that the solicitor assessed that there would be no defence, and there was a relatively high chance of an action being raised. This risk, combined with the fact that it was relatively easy to remove the material, led to the recommendation that it be removed. The second occasion concerned a headline that the news editor for *Reporting Scotland*[7] wanted to lead with one night: 'Trustee Admits Misappropriation', after the Lord Advocate, in a court action to remove some trustees from a charitable trust, had produced in court a letter written by the trustee which he alleged supported his case. The solicitor advised that the headline be toned down so that it not be presented as a matter of fact, but of allegation. This resulted in the down-grading of the story within the news bulletin.

Conclusions on rewriting material

The level of rewriting required by the solicitor depends upon the extent to which he or she is involved in the production of the article or programme. The BBC solicitor becomes involved at a much earlier stage in the production of the material than the newspaper solicitors, and is therefore able to adopt a more hands-on approach. His immediate availability in the BBC building may encourage this. The solicitor for the evening local paper is more involved than the solicitor for the national daily, since potentially troublesome material is routinely sent to him, even while in the course of investigation. The national daily, on the other hand, routinely screens only completed stories which are checked by lawyers shortly before the newspaper goes into production. All three solicitors reported that the journalists with whom they work have a high level of awareness of the law of defamation, and two of them, indeed, take part in training programmes for new journalists. This means that the material the solicitors see has already been subject to editorial and journalistic censoring in the light of the law of defamation.

---

[7] The early evening news bulletin, broadcast immediately after the *Six O'Clock News*.

Relations between legal advisers and editors

The questions here were designed to see how far editors are willing to dispute or disregard advice that they receive from their legal advisers. All three interviewees reported very good relationships with the editorial teams they work with, and this was reflected in the discussion with editors. The solicitor for the national daily reported no disagreements at all during the time frame. The solicitor for the evening local paper made this comment in response to the question of how often his advice is ignored:

It's a question of confidence. But that's the same whatever type of lawyer you are. If they have confidence in you and know that they can trust you they will take your advice and mostly they do. But lawyers are cautious. It is not for me to assess the risks. I tell them what the risks are and they decide whether to take the risk. But if I make suggestions they nearly always follow them.

The solicitor for BBC Scotland replied:

It is very rare for us to have disagreements. We can usually accommodate each other quite happily. We don't tend to have disagreements as such, but there have been one or two small occasions when I've had to argue my corner. There was a case a week or two ago when the Gaelic team wanted to do a piece about adulterated Romanian wine which seems to have been polluted due to proximity to a chemical factory. Though the manufacturers are Romanian we could potentially have a verbal injury[8] claim, and I had to persuade them of the risk. I managed.

We conclude that as in any solicitor–client relationship, the willingness of the client to take the solicitor's advice depends on the level of trust between the two. A few years prior to this study the same firm of solicitors was used by both the newspapers covered by this study, but there was some radical disagreement

---

[8] Malicious falsehood in England. The claim could have been based on what is called in both legal systems slander of trade or slander of property.

between one editor and solicitor and now the newspapers are advised by different solicitors. The strong (admittedly personal) impression gained is that the character of each solicitor interviewed suits very well the character of the newspaper he or she represents. This feature, which can be seen at the BBC as well, would seem to play a large part in the harmony of the relations which was uniformly reported between solicitors and editors.

Risk factors

The question of which factors are particularly significant in assessing the riskiness of a particular item or story was asked of both editors and solicitors. A variety of interesting responses was given.

The solicitors were all primarily concerned with whether the truth of the story could be proved to the satisfaction of the court. They clearly had in mind the rule of law that the onus of proving truth rests squarely with the defender. There were many difficulties identified in judging the truthfulness of a story and whether it could be proved. For one thing many stories come from agencies which makes it impossible for the newspaper to check the facts. In other cases reporters generally know that they should check at least two sources. From the lawyer's point of view, it was said to be particularly important to be told as much as possible in order to judge whether truth could be proved.

Other risks include the risk that the statement might have a defamatory meaning, though interestingly a number of people suggested that the Scottish courts are rather less likely to hold a statement to have a defamatory meaning than the English courts are. Certainly there are no examples in the Scottish law reports of successful claims being made where there is serious doubt whether the statement is anything more than personally hurtful and there is a clear impression amongst Scottish practitioners that the English courts are more willing to accept that merely hurtful statements are in themselves defamatory. One highly experienced legal adviser stated that innuendo is almost never used by potential pursuers in Scotland and that the vast majority of complaints unambiguously point to some fact which is claimed to be inaccurate. This perception, whether it is true or not, has perhaps encouraged defenders' advisers to be more robust in rejecting out of hand obviously spurious claims than they would be in England.

The chances of being sued are assessed according to the perceived character of the individual who may have been defamed. This point was raised by a number of people, both editorial and legal, as a very significant factor. It was stated to be well-known that the late Robert Maxwell 'terrorized' the English press, and while only one of those interviewed had dealt with that individual, every solicitor in the project could give similar, though less extreme, examples. The case of the sensitive explorer has already been mentioned. MPs were also cited by one editor as a fertile source of complaints (though seldom writs).

One risk that was mentioned by editors, though less by solicitors, was the chance of being sued in England. This affects the assessment of risk because the damages that can be awarded by the courts there is, as already mentioned, so much greater. One editor rather bitterly commented that English courts award 'Danegeld', and that 'you just can't trust English juries'. Clearly the assessment of risks lies in the hands of editors rather than solicitors; the solicitors see their role as explaining what the risk is, leaving it to the editor to determine whether, economically, it is worth taking. It is more of a live issue for cross-border broadcasts, and was expressly mentioned as a matter of concern by the solicitor who acts for Borders Television. Since the rules of jurisdiction are fairly liberal in England (see Chapter 1 above) it is perhaps surprising that this is not more of a concern for publishers who have offices in England (as all those investigated in this study do) and even tiny circulations there. The English courts have held that this is sufficient to give them jurisdiction, and the fact that this is not perceived as a significant risk factor other than in obvious cases may suggest that financial gain is rather less of a motivation for pursuers than the vindication of their reputations in the place where their reputations exist. One well-known case illustrates this. In 1989 both Channel 4 and Scottish Television broadcast allegations that Mr A. Gecas, a long-term resident in Edinburgh, was a Lithuanian war criminal. He sued Scottish Television in Edinburgh but did not sue Channel 4 in London.[9] An alternative explanation is that many defamatory allegations are repeated in more than one media outlet and the pursuer may therefore have a choice not only of which jurisdiction to sue in but also of which defender to sue. This may have the effect of diverting cases away from Scottish defenders as well as Scottish courts. If, however, there is a realistic chance of being sued in England, the institution is likely to be much more ready to settle. The case of *Foxen* v. *Scotsman Publications* was mentioned in Chapter 1. That was the case in which the English court held that it had jurisdiction over a newspaper 90 per cent of the circulation of which was in Scotland, and it is interesting to note that the claim was settled shortly after the English court accepted jurisdiction.

Editors are also very conscious of the need to weigh up the relative importance of particular stories with the costs of defending it. They might be willing to take more of a risk with a story of some significance than with a story with no real importance. One editor reported holding back a story about one trade-union official calling another a liar, not because he disbelieved that the official was a liar but because it would take up more resources finding verifiable proof of the fact than could be justified by the importance of the story.

Court Actions

The final set of questions concerned the number of writs that had been received by each organization in the relevant periods, court

---

[9] In the event, the defenders' plea of *veritas* (justification in England) was upheld.

appearances, and consultations. Reflecting the generally small number of claims in Scotland, the answers showed very limited activity here. No-one reported having sought counsel's opinion during the period under investigation, for the simple reason that there is no specialist defamation bar in Scotland, and the solicitors involved are at least as experienced in defamation work as any member of the Faculty of Advocates. One solicitor said that his English newspaper clients sometimes insist on counsel's opinion, because that is expected in England, but in his view this was a complete waste of money since he himself does more defamation work than anyone in Parliament House. The only use of advocates is when a case goes to the Court of Session which has restricted rights of audience. The BBC will commonly use an advocate in oral arguments in the Sheriff Court, where solicitors have a right of audience, though their own solicitor will appear in the preliminary stages. Within the periods under investigation, the solicitor for the local evening paper appeared in court once, though only to fix a date for the next preliminary hearing, and the solicitor for the BBC appeared for two procedural hearings. Contact with the Faculty of Advocates is limited to giving instructions, and not consultation.

As far as the number of writs issued is concerned, there were no writs served against the national daily during the period of the study, one served against the local evening paper, and one served against the BBC. Many more letters of complaint were dealt with by letters between legal advisers.

Why there are fewer claims in Scotland

The question here was why the number of claims in Scotland should be so much less than in England. Obviously the answers were impressionistic and to some extent anecdotal, since no-one had done any study into this question. But everyone who was asked the question had some opinion to express, and they had all thought about it before hand. Interestingly, all the solicitors reported an increase in defamation work from about the late

1980s, and this was blamed on the high-profile (and high-damages) cases from the English courts which are given national coverage.

One solicitor gave this rather surprising answer:

> The lawyers in Scotland are more sensible than in England. They give better advice at the start and Scottish newspapers are more responsible. Take the *Daily Record*.[10] That's a tabloid but the editor is realistic and he knows what he can and cannot print. He is not prepared to publish material that he cannot defend.

He then suggested that some English tabloids take a far less responsible attitude.

Other people pointed out that few solicitors in Scotland do much defamation work, and this makes legal advisers much more willing to negotiate and compromise. One solicitor admitted having been able on at least one occasion to knock a case out of court during the stage of preliminary legal argument through the inexperience of the pursuer's solicitor. Also, there are far fewer very wealthy people in Scotland who are willing and able to take the matter to court if they are not offered a settlement that satisfies them: it was said 'the people who threaten to sue don't actually want to sue. They want to settle.' More than one person suggested that the Scots are generally less litigious than the English.

Every solicitor to whom we spoke claimed that people who sue in Scotland genuinely do not want money as much as they want their reputations restored. All had done some pursuer work. One suggestion was that newspapers are more competitive in England, encouraging the taking of risks more there than in Scotland. Another claimed that the main reason (other than the different levels of damages) was the fact that the English courts are much more ready to draw a defamatory innuendo while in Scotland the court seems to require factual allegations. He went on to suggest

---

[10] This is a national tabloid, the best selling in Scotland and the only one edited and produced in Scotland.

that this position can be explained by the fact that there is no one in the Scottish legal profession who specializes in looking for and finding defamatory innuendos upon which to found convoluted claims. The latter point is certainly correct, though there is little hard evidence from the law reports that the Scottish courts take a tougher line on innuendo than the English courts. An example given by both the editor and his solicitor (independently of each other) to illustrate this point was a complaint made by a public figure who was described in the newspaper as 'a member of the Scottish Conservative Party'. Though this reference was factually untrue, the newspaper refused to print an apology and denied vehemently that any defamatory innuendo could be drawn from the statement. Various solicitors' letters passed between the parties, but no writ was served. Another example was given by the solicitor for the local evening newspaper:

We had a claim yesterday concerning a report in the *Evening Times* of a murder of a 17 year old boy and the article said that the mother lived in Edinburgh and that the police had taken 24 hours to locate her and tell her that her son had been killed. The mother's solicitor wrote to me yesterday to say that it was grossly defamatory to say that his client lived in Edinburgh and that it had taken 24 hours to locate her. She lived around the corner from where the murder happened. The solicitor claims that she is distressed because of these inaccuracies and what are our proposals for compensation? This is completely spurious. It's absurd. The report was clearly wrong, because the woman did live round the corner and had been contacted straight away. But to argue that it sounds in damages to make these mistakes is nonsense. We will publish an apology but probably not at the moment since it looks like there is some evidentiary importance to the murder trial in where the mother was.

Willingness to settle

Questions were also directed to how willing parties were to settle a claim. All solicitors reported that they rejected out of hand clearly spurious claims. They were willing to settle when the allegation was clearly wrong, clearly defamatory, and there was no other defence. Some organizations were more unwilling to settle than others in the more complicated cases that fall between the clearly spurious and the clearly defamatory, and it is here that the issues mentioned in the section above headed *Risk factors* come into play. There is a widespread unwillingness to publish apologies, though retractions of factual errors are more common.

The solicitor for the national daily newspaper reported that she spent most of her time on negotiating settlements. The editors have final say on whether to settle or not, but the solicitors do the negotiating. She said this: 'The vast majority of my work is in negotiation. Both sides want to settle. Nobody in their right mind goes to court in this area of the law. It's different if the case comes from England.'

Insurance

Insurance against defamation is not common in Scotland, though not everyone spoken to was willing to answer questions on this matter. The Scotsman Publications Ltd, which produces a large number of newspapers and periodicals, national and local, are, perhaps surprisingly, not insured against defamation claims. This no doubt reflects an assessment that the costs of such insurance outweighs the risk of having to pay out substantial amounts. Their solicitor tied in this question to the lack of in-house lawyers in Scotland: 'If an organisation like *The Scotsman Publications Ltd* used an in-house lawyer who then made a mistake, they would have no-one to sue. If they use an outside lawyer, like me, then my mistakes give them access to the solicitor's indemnity fund.'

An independent radio producer, who produces programmes for BBC Radio Scotland, and who in fifteen years reports 'never having had a whiff of a complaint', carries no insurance, though his contract with the BBC obliges him to produce no material of an obscene or defamatory nature. He interprets this clause as allowing him access to the BBC Scotland solicitor for advice during the production stage.

Conclusions

Everyone who was spoken to agreed that the law of defamation in Scotland has a chilling effect and inhibits what newspapers and broadcasters feel able to publish. Though the number of claims is very much lower in Scotland than in England there is no evidence to suggest that editors in Scotland take the threat any less seriously. There is nothing to suggest that Scottish publishers take more risks than English publishers, and, if anything, the popular end of the newspaper market in Scotland is less sensationalist and less willing to take risks than its English counterpart (even although the financial consequence of the risk going wrong is very much less). This may well provide an answer to those who claim that the law of defamation, as it operates in England, is necessary to restrain the excesses of an unscrupulous press whose only motivation is profit. The financial consequences of defamation are less significant in Scotland than in England, but this has not led to the Scottish media being more cavalier than their English counterparts. One implication may be that editors are influenced by a range of social and cultural attitudes, including, but not confined to, a desire to avoid complaints arising from the publication of defamatory material. These are more important than the draconian rules of defamation law, among them the possibility of a large damages award, in curbing undesirable journalistic practices.

Nearly everyone interviewed made another interesting point. The law of contempt is regarded as a far more dangerous area of the law for the Scottish media. There are a number of reasons for this. For one thing the legal wrong is criminal rather than civil, which could result in imprisonment for the editor rather than damages against the company. There is more chance of an adverse judgment harming the organization's reputation, and there is no appeal to the House of Lords in a Scottish criminal case. Most people also stated as a fact that the Scottish courts are far stricter in their interpretation of the laws of contempt than the English courts, making the risk so much greater. One solicitor also suggested that a certain kudos is obtained from a defamation claim in the sense that the organization can say that it is investigative and is not afraid of the establishment, while with contempt all that can be said is that the organization is interfering with the course of justice.

All in all, there is no doubt of the inhibiting effect of the law of defamation on the media in Scotland, even when all parties are perfectly aware that the financial risks are relatively minor compared to south of the Border. There are far fewer claims, but not, it would seem, fewer fears than in England, and the effect of the law on the practice of the media is not significantly different between the two jurisdictions.

9

Conclusions

Introduction

In this final Chapter we draw some general conclusions from our study. First, we summarize our findings about the different impact the law of defamation has on the various branches of the media, and then draw some conclusions which seem to be equally valid for all branches. Secondly, we offer some observations on the question of the 'chilling effect' of this area of law on media freedom, the investigation of which was one of our principal aims in embarking on the research. Lastly, we make a few remarks concerning the significance of our findings for reform of the law of defamation. These are made very tentatively. In the first place, it was not our object to make a case for legislative reform. More importantly the decision to reform libel law should follow an assessment of the appropriate balance between media freedom and the interest individuals have in protecting their reputation; only if the present law does not strike the balance in an appropriate way should it be amended. But our research did not look at the concerns of plaintiffs. It does however highlight the particular respects in which the law creates difficulties for the media, and perhaps puts one or two matters on the law reform agenda.

The Differential Impact of Libel Law on the Media

Although we found that all branches of the media, both in England and in Scotland, are concerned about the implications of libel law for their activities, there are significant differences in the levels of this impact. At one end of the scale are the national newspapers (see Chapter 3). They clearly find the law of libel irksome, and they take considerable trouble to minimize its risks by rewriting stories, etc., but they rarely refrain from covering a story altogether or water one down significantly. There is evidence that some tabloids will carry stories with known libel risks owing to the fear that otherwise their rivals will have exclusive coverage or because the stories are just too good to ignore; it is a nice question whether this on occasion amounts to reckless behaviour. We should emphasize that we did not get the same impression from the more serious broadsheets. Equally, budgetary and financial considerations do not appear to exercise significant constraints on the national press, at any rate in taking the initial decision whether to publish the story or not. They do, however, as with all the other media, enter into the difficult calculation whether it is right to settle or fight proceedings. Many national newspapers do not take out libel insurance, and are therefore wholly uninfluenced by insurance costs. Some London papers do carry, or have carried, libel insurance, but the excess is so high that they rarely rely on it. Rising premiums and the pressure of insurance companies (or their solicitors) to settle claims do not appear important factors in their calculations, another difference as will be seen from some other media sectors.

At the other end of the spectrum are book publishers, magazines, and the regional press. All these media feel acutely vulnerable to the impact of libel law, and admit that their decision whether to publish a story may be influenced by the fear of libel proceedings. However, this caution may be induced by a variety of factors. We found that regional newspapers are sensitive about their own standing in the community and do not wish to acquire a reputation for publishing unjustifiable attacks on local personalities. Often editors take personal responsibility for dealing with a complaint and sending an apology when appropriate. But equally regional papers are influenced by the costs of contesting a libel action; even a modest sum paid by way of settlement and legal costs might necessitate savings in the editorial budget or, it was claimed, conceivably spell financial ruin (see Chapter 4). Book publishers, with generally low profit margins, were also constrained by the financial problems arising from a delayed publication date or, even worse, a withdrawn title. Additionally, (as explained in Chapter 6) a book publisher is exposed to the risk of legal proceedings brought several years after the initial publication date, and it is not practicable for him, as it is for most other media outlets, to deal with a complaint by inserting an apology in another issue (or on another day in the programme schedule). Both book and magazine publishers are vulnerable because of the threat that a writ may be issued against distributors, booksellers, and newsagents who have no interest of principle in defending proceedings and who may be willing to withdraw a title and/or pay agreed compensation to the prejudice of the book or periodical publisher. Magazine publishers (see Chapter 7) have for the most part little interest in publishing a 'hot' story for the sake of it, or challenging, say, a particular politician or City figure to sue it—though this proposition does not apply of course to campaigning or satirical magazines such as the *New Statesman* or *Private Eye*.

Perhaps broadcasters should be located in the middle of this spectrum, though it is hard to pinpoint exactly where. Some of them, such as the BBC and the larger commercial companies, e.g., Channel 4 and Granada, are similar to the national press in so far as they are committed to investigative journalism and to providing the public with comprehensive news. On the other hand, their culture is quite different, in that they are already subject to a relatively tight legal regime operated by the Independent Television Commission and the Broadcasting Complaints Commission (from 1997 the Broadcasting Standards Commission). Moreover, we found that lawyers may become involved at an early stage of programme preparation to monitor it for libel risks, that some programmes are automatically previewed for the same purpose, and that on occasion prospective plaintiffs put editors and channel controllers under considerable pressure to remove particular allegations. For obvious reasons, as discussed in Chapter 5, broadcasters are particularly liable to actions for unintentional defamation—for an accidental reference to an actual person or company in a fictional drama or for showing in the course of a film about, say, police corruption, the face of someone wholly uninvolved in the matter. Only broadcasters, so far as we know, employ people to check registers and lists to avoid this problem, though book publishers, and to some extent newspapers, mentioned the same difficulty which in principle confronts all branches of the media.

One feature which distinguishes (most) national newspapers and many broadcasting companies (in particular the BBC and Channel 4) from the overwhelming majority of book and periodical publishers and regional papers is that the former employ in-house lawyers. We have concluded that this is an important factor. In-house lawyers, as they themselves admitted, see their primary function as that of assisting the journalists and editors to get the story out, albeit in a way which minimizes libel risks. They share the culture of their employer, whether that is the BBC or a major newspaper group. They denied that they ever acted as censors and emphasized the essentially co-operative character of their work with journalist colleagues. In contrast, our impression is that frequently outside lawyers take a more legalistic stance, stressing the risks of successful libel proceedings unless the media can justify the story with convincing evidence. It is impossible to quantify the significance of this point, but we were struck by it in a number of interviews. It is perhaps inevitable that an outside lawyer working in private practice, however sympathetic to the media, will have a different perspective from that of a newspaper or broadcasting employee. Against this, it should be emphasized that a solicitor's *advice* is just that, and we heard that on occasion editors do decide to ignore it.

Other institutional factors influence the conduct of various media players. With the national and the regional press the editor has the final word, though it is relatively rare for the editor of a Fleet Street paper to become involved in the same way as the editor of a regional paper. In contrast, with many periodicals the general manager may determine in conjunction with the editor whether to publish a controversial article, and the decision is therefore likely to be influenced by financial considerations. In the case of broadcasting companies we have found that exceptionally controversial documentaries and current affairs programmes (though obviously not news) may be referred up the hierarchy to senior officials before a decision is taken whether to transmit the item or not; it seems likely that financial consideration enter into the calculation whether to take a risk or not, as was admitted by some of our interviewees. We found little evidence of this with the national press.

It seems clear that defamation law in practice poses less of a problem in Scotland. That, too, may be partly attributable to institutional factors, in particular, the absence of specialist firms of solicitors and a libel Bar. But that itself is almost certainly the consequence of a different attitude to defamation actions and the absence of a large number of wealthy potential plaintiffs (see Chapter 8). But distinctions between English and Scottish law and procedure are also significant: damages are much lower in Scotland, where exemplary damages are not accepted, while jury trial is very rare. It seems that Scots lawyers are less keen to strain the words to discover a possible defamatory meaning, a danger of which some journalists and media lawyers in London are very aware. Scots lawyers are particularly wary of the risks of a libel action south of the Border in respect of a Scottish newspaper or broadcast also distributed or received in England.

Some Common Conclusions

The last point in the previous paragraph is relevant to one general conclusion which applies to all media sectors: uncertainty in both the principles of defamation law and their practical application induce great caution on the part of the media. Virtually every interviewee, in all branches of the media, emphasized the lottery aspect attached to this area of the law. First, it may be unclear how a person or company will react to a story which with some ingenuity might be understood to carry a defamatory meaning. Every story, script, and film must be checked and redrafted or retaken to avoid the risk of such an interpretation. Secondly, although a complaint may be made or a writ served, it may not be pursued for a variety of reasons. National newspaper and broadcasting lawyers both pointed to the high proportion of dormant writs, cases which have gone to sleep for months or years. But the files cannot be destroyed, and cases can be reactivated quite suddenly at a time when the media lawyer is no longer in contact with key witnesses.

Finally, the decision whether to settle or contest a case is itself a gamble, even after taking (quite expensive) outside legal advice. Media-company lawyers identified a number of legal and financial questions relevant to that decision: does the plaintiff have the means or the financial backing to pursue the case to the final stage; what is the quality of the evidence; in particular will the sources for the story disappear or refuse to give evidence; and, most crucially, how will the jury react to the respective arguments; and what level of damages might it award? A large number of interviewees stressed that trial by jury necessarily made a case unpredictable; there was a widespread feeling that juries are biassed against the media, particularly the national press. As a consequence cases were not contested unless it was really felt that they could be won because of the weight of the evidence and the reliability of witnesses prepared to testify for the defendant. We found no evidence for the view that the media are sometimes prepared to fight 'poor' cases to defend press freedom. For those media with insurance there was some evidence that regional papers, broadcasters, or publishers do on occasion come under pressure from their insurers to settle cases which the newspaper or other media outlet is confident it could fight. However, that was not the majority view of regional newspaper editors.

It is also unpredictable how much a jury will award by way of damages, another point made by many of our interviewees. Scots lawyers repeatedly stressed that this was the major reason they feared an action in the English courts. It is likely there will be greater consistency in jury awards after the *Elton John* case[1] (see Chapter 1), but equally it would be wrong to expect the development of a tariff system (e.g., £1,000 for a nominal libel, £20,000 as a moderate award, and £100,000 for serious cases) equivalent to that which regulates personal injuries damages. Several interviewees (particularly regional newspaper editors and book publishers) said that insurance premiums had increased significantly after a handful of well-publicized high awards had been made in the last five years. In this context it is interesting that some Scottish solicitors reported an increase in defamation work in the wake of these English cases.

We would add a few other conclusions about the common media experience of defamation law. First, interviewees from all sectors—and in both jurisdictions—expressed particular concern about the propensity of police officers to sue for libel. It was widely felt that this had reached the point that some outlets, in particular regional papers, had more or less abandoned writing stories with allegations of excessive force or brutality on the part of the police. Some anxiety was expressed about the litigiousness of particular individuals (the name of Robert Maxwell was frequently mentioned) or companies, but the Police Federation and Scottish Police Federation (and those they represent) seem unique in their capacity to induce caution on the part of editors and broadcasters. Secondly, every media lawyer testified to the difficulty of justifying allegations in court, and their constant need to bring this point home to journalists and editors. Various difficulties were mentioned: witnesses might die or simply disappear, while others would prove unreliable when it came to giving evidence several years after the events around which the allegations centred. Some witnesses, e.g., members or supporters of terrorist organizations, are so lacking in credibility that their

---

[1] [1996] 1 All ER 35.

evidence is discounted in advance when deciding whether their allegations can be published.

Finally, almost all the people we spoke to expressed concern about the legal and other costs of libel law. Indeed, for many of our interviewees this was much the most disturbing aspect to a defamation claim. There was quite detailed evidence about the recent rise in insurance premiums affecting regional newspaper groups and book and periodical publishers (see Chapters 4, 6, and 7), and we gained some impression of the costs of libel for major broadcasting companies (see Chapter 5). National newspapers, as we have frequently had occasion to observe, were much less helpful in this respect, though they were anxious to say in broad terms that the costs are considerable. Whether that is objectively so or not, they are clearly *perceived* to be high. This is one reason why many media companies are reluctant to go for outside legal advice if the matter can be resolved by an in-house lawyer. Further, it was put forward by respondents in all sectors as a reason for settling many claims which might be defended successfully: it is often not worth fighting a case even though the story is believed to be accurate. A newspaper or broadcaster may consider it preferable in some circumstances to pay a persistent complainant a few thousand pounds to go away rather than face a mounting legal bill and an uncertain outcome if the case came to court. We feel that this is a matter which requires further research. In particular, it would be interesting to discover whether libel costs are excessive compared to the equivalent costs of contesting personal injuries or other civil cases.

The Chilling Effect of Defamation Law

As we have said at various points in this book (see for instance Preface, Chapter 1 at pp. 14–15, and Chapter 2 at p. 32) the media frequently argue that their freedom to publish material of real public interest is deterred or chilled by defamation law. The term 'chilling effect' is of American legal origin, developed by the US Supreme Court in a number of areas of free-speech law and applied to libel cases.[2] It refers to the effect of the rules of law, whether criminal or civil, and of official practices on the exercise of freedom of speech and of the media. Administrative censorship and court injunctions prevent publication in an immediate and straightforward manner. In contrast, the threat of a criminal prosecution or a civil action for damages may deter the media from publishing a story, even though if a prosecution (or action) were brought, the press (or other media outlet) would be able to defend the action.

The law of libel exercises a chilling effect, it is said, because the defences of justification, fair comment, and privilege do not adequately safeguard the interest of the media (and the public) in freedom of expression. The media may, for instance, be unsure whether they could prove the truth of the allegations in court or, even if confident on that score, they may be concerned by the legal cost of defending an action brought by a wealthy and persistent litigant. It was for these reasons that the US Supreme Court held that the common law of libel was incompatible with the First Amendment guarantee of freedom of speech and of the press.[3] It found that to put the burden of proving truth (or showing fair comment) on the media would inevitably deter the dissemination of truth. Its conclusion has been well summarized by a leading American commentator on defamation law:[4] 'Because of the risks and uncertainties in the process of ascertaining and demonstrating factual truth, a rule that penalizes factual falsity has the effect of inducing some self-censorship as to materials *that are in fact true*.' The House of Lords has recently accepted that the law of defamation may chill freedom of political discussion when it ruled that a public authority lacks title to sue in libel;[5] it

---

[2] For the origins of the principle, see the anonymous student note, 'The Chilling Effect in Constitutional Law' (1969) 69 *Col. L Rev.* 802.

[3] *New York Times* v. *Sullivan*, 376 US 254 (1964).

[4] F. Schauer, 'Social Foundations of the Law of Defamation—A Comparative Analysis', (1980) 1 *Jo. of Media Law & Practice* 3, 11 (author's emphasis).

[5] *Derbyshire County Council* v. *Times Newspapers Ltd* [1993] AC 534: see Ch. 1, p. 6.

remains to be seen whether the principle will applied (as in Australia, see Chapter 1) to limit the ability of politicians to take proceedings to protect their reputation.

This study has attempted to move beyond legal principle to an account of social (and socio-legal) practice. We believe that our investigation of the impact of defamation law on various media has demonstrated clearly that the chilling effect in this area genuinely does exist and significantly restricts what the public is able to read and hear. The basis for this judgement has, we hope, been established in the preceding chapters. Additionally, however, our findings have led us to the conclusion that, whilst the idea of the chilling effect is entirely valid, it requires some reformulation to reflect fully the complexity of the ways in which its pernicious effects are actually brought about.

The most obvious manifestation, which may be called the *direct* chilling effect, occurs when articles, books, or programmes are specifically changed in light of legal considerations. Most often perhaps this takes the form of omission of material the author believes to be true but cannot establish to the extent judged sufficient to avoid an unacceptable risk of legal action and an award of damages. This produces the attitude exemplified by most magazine editors and publishers (see Chapter 7): 'if in doubt, strike it out'. 'Doubt' here, it should be emphasized, relates to their ability to present a legally sustainable defence, not to the editor's view of the validity of the story. In addition, passages may be rewritten to alter meaning, remove an innuendo, or recast statements of fact into those of opinion. These responses are all possible because the risk is visible—literally on the desk or computer monitor of the editor or lawyer whose job it is to consider the libel risk posed by specific material before it is released to the public. Hence the work of editing and 'legalling' for libel is one of the processes directly shaping the finished product. This conscious inhibition, or self-censorship within the organization, remains hidden from the public who are unaware of how their television programme, book, or newspaper is actually produced. And one of our main findings is that the impact of the direct chilling effect is not at all uniform. Different media experience it with notably different force. For reasons we have explored, it bears far more heavily on book publishers, broadcasters, and the regional press than on the national press, where its impact seems relatively minor.

However, there is another, deeper, and subtler way in which libel inhibits media publication. This may be called the *structural* chilling effect. It is not manifest through alteration or cancellation of a specific article, programme, or book. Rather it functions in a preventive manner: preventing the creation of certain material. Particular organizations and individuals are considered taboo because of the libel risk; certain subjects are treated as off-limits, minefields into which it is too dangerous to stray. Nothing is edited to lessen libel risk because nothing is written in the first place.

By its very nature, the structural chilling effect is far more difficult to quantify, and even to pinpoint, than the direct effect. In our study, it was manifest perhaps most clearly in the conscious decision taken by some publishing firms to refuse as a matter of policy to commission certain categories of books (see Chapter 6). Yet in every branch of the media there were numerous indications of the existence of 'no-go areas', which we have described in each of the relevant chapters. And in this respect, unlike the direct chilling effect, there is no indication that the national press is any less affected. Preventive self-censorship seems just as effective in ensuring that journalists and editors on these newspapers steer well clear of, for example, investigations of deaths in police custody; exploitative employment practices by various large companies operating in the United Kingdom; or bribery and other corrupt practices by British companies bidding for overseas contracts. The structural chilling effect narrows the range of what is thought publishable, and may even remove certain topics altogether from exposure and public scrutiny.

A secondary form of structural chilling effect may be discerned, if less clearly. It is best encapsulated by the remark of a journalist on a national broadsheet, quoted in Chapter 3, who suggested that the libel laws had made the British press more 'polemical'—by which he meant the antithesis of factually-orientated—than it otherwise might be. If true, this is a good example of the functional application of legal rules, as understood by those who operate under them. The key point is that, whilst the defence of justification in effect requires proof of the truth of any seriously discreditable allegation,[6] that of fair comment is a little more generous from the point of view of the media. Though it would be over-simple (and, in terms of libel risk, dangerously inaccurate) for a journalist or author to act on the belief that he is safe so long as he recasts allegations of fact into statements of opinion, outside egregious cases the risk undoubtedly would be lessened in so far as he is able to do this. The rule that comment need only be shown to be fair by reference to those facts proved to be true, though these may have been accompanied by other false statements, obviously gives more leeway to expressions of opinion. If allegations of fact can be expressed in the form of hints or ambiguous suggestions, so much the better—but also, for good journalism, so much the worse. Writing in these terms interposes a greater distance between the writer and the particular state of affairs he purports to describe, and can only reduce the credibility of his expressions of opinion in the mind of a thoughtful reader.

On this view, the approach of journalists to their craft has been influenced by the way in which they are allowed to say things: it is safer to write opaquely or make comment than it is to engage in clear and hard-edged investigative journalism. The idea that the style of the press, and possibly of other media, has been moulded at least in significant measure by the law of defamation is not empirically testable, but none the less has a ring of truth to it.

---

[6] As was seen in Ch. 1, the Defamation Act 1952, s. 5, provides that a defence of justification is not to fail because inaccurate details are added to allegations which are shown to be true. It is unclear whether juries, and for that matter journalists, always understand this subtlety.

Clearly insufficient on its own, it may go some way to explaining why much British journalism lacks serious content.[7]

Reform of Libel Law

Our research highlights a number of causes of dissatisfaction on the part of the media with the operation of the present libel law. Disquiet is, it appears, more strongly felt in England than in Scotland, though we would not want to minimize the impact of defamation law north of the Border, where it is as relevant to editorial decision-making as it is in England. We discuss these matters under separate headings with a few tentative suggestions on how the law might be reformed to meet this disquiet. However, as we have already emphasized in the opening paragraph of this chapter, our findings do not establish a knock-down case for reform; at most they show a possible direction for radical reform of the defamation law if the judgement is made that it does not strike an appropriate balance between the interests of plaintiffs in protecting their reputation and the interests of the media, and the public, in freedom of expression.

1. Unintentional defamation

We have drawn attention to the steps taken by broadcasters in order to minimize the risk of liability to someone of whose existence they are entirely unaware—through use of the name of an existing person in a drama or by accidentally including him in a film. Book publishers (as shown by a recent notorious example mentioned in Chapter 6) and newspapers are also exposed to liability for defaming someone inadvertently, though in practice this is less of a problem for them. Liability for unintentional defamation was established by the House of Lords in *Hulton* v. *Jones*[8] and has remained a firm principle of the common law since

---

[7] Another factor is almost certainly the absence of a legally enforceable right to privacy, a feature of the common law which sits oddly with its strong concern to protect the right to reputation.   [8] [1910] AC 20: see Ch. 1.

then. But it is arguably an anomalous rule in the context of a system of civil liability which generally requires a plaintiff to prove that the defendant was at fault or negligent.

As explained in Chapter 1, the defence of an offer of amends for unintentional defamation (under the 1952 legislation) was very little used. The expanded defence under the Defamation Act 1996 covers this type of case, though if, say, a broadcaster's offer is accepted, it will still have to pay damages, albeit to be assessed by a judge and not a jury. It is unclear whether media defendants will be more willing to use the defence than they were its predecessor.

Arguably, it is bizarre to require broadcasters to go to the lengths they do to minimize the chance of liability for unintentional defamation. Negative checking of reference books and lists of addresses surely goes beyond the taking of reasonable precautions required in other areas of the law. Other media outlets do not have the time or facilities to engage in this burdensome activity. There is perhaps a case for requiring a plaintiff to show that the libel was published negligently with regard to him or her, that is, the media outlet should have known that it might be understood by reasonable readers to refer to him/her.

2. Burden of proof

In recent years there has been some discussion of the burden of proof in libel law, though an amendment moved in the House of Lords Committee stage of the recent Defamation Bill to put the onus on the plaintiff to show falsity was defeated.[9] There is a presumption of falsity in the common law of both England and Scotland, so that any factual allegations must be substantiated by the defendant if it is to escape liability. We have pointed out in this Chapter and at various points in the book the considerable difficulties media (and other) defendants may have in establishing truth. Awareness of these difficulties, at all levels in a media

[9] The amendment was moved by Lord Lester of Herne Hill, QC: see 571 HL Deb. cols. 239–243.

enterprise, produces the 'chilling effect' analysed in the previous section.

Quite apart from the compatibility of the presumption of falsity with freedom of speech,[10] one can doubt whether it is reasonable to expect the defendant to show the truth of matters, in the nature of things generally outside his personal knowledge, rather than require the plaintiff to show the allegations are false. After all the plaintiff will always know the truth about his or her conduct. The New South Wales Law Reform Commission has concluded that 'as a practical matter, it makes sense to put the burden of proof of falsity on the plaintiff simply because the plaintiff, "who knows the truth", is more likely to be in a position to prove falsity than the defendant to prove truth'.[11] We consider there is enough substance in this conclusion to warrant further consideration of the matter in English and Scots law.

3. The role of the jury in assessing damages

One conclusion, applicable to all media sectors in England, is that the unpredictability of jury awards of damages reduces many decisions pertinent to libel to a lottery. This is particularly the case with regard to the post-complaint and writ stage when the key questions are whether, and when, to settle a case, and on what terms. It is only right to point out that plaintiffs face the same quandary, though for the media this is a continuing anxiety, an inescapable aspect of their daily activity. It is worth adding that in Scotland there is a greater alarm over libel risks when it is apprehended that there may be an action in England—largely because of the phenomenon of jury trial in the latter jurisdiction (see Chapter 8).

The role of the jury in libel cases raises fundamental, even

---

[10] See E. Barendt, 'Libel and Freedom of Speech in English Law' [1993] *Public Law* 449.   [11] Report 75 (1995), para. 4.20.

constitutional questions[12] which of course are outside the scope of this study. There are powerful arguments for jury determination of questions relating to meaning and whether the defences are made out. However, it is clear that the unpredictability of their awards, at least in conjunction with the scale of legal costs, makes the decision whether to fight a case in the courts or to settle it much of a gamble. (Indeed, we consider the concern expressed by the media, and probably also felt by plaintiffs, about the costs of fighting a libel action to be sufficiently significant to warrant a separate study.) The Faulks Committee in 1975 recommended that the role of the jury in assessing damages should be confined to stating whether the award to be made by the judge should be substantial, moderate, nominal, or contemptuous.[13] However, there are practical difficulties in keeping separate the functions of judge and jury in this context. Moreover, the recent decision in the *Elton John* case is likely to lead to more predictable (and lower) awards which may do much to reduce the lottery element in handling a defamation claim. If this does not prove to be the case, our findings provide some support for the argument for looking again at the role of the jury in awarding damages—though we would add that the unpredictability of their decisions is only one element in the libel lottery.

---

[12] See for instance the judgment of Nourse LJ in *Sutcliffe* v. *Pressdram* [1991] 1 QB 153, 181–3.   [13] Cmnd. 5909, para. 512.

Index